CONTEMPORARY CAREER
DEVELOPMENT ISSUES

SERIES IN APPLIED PSYCHOLOGY

Edwin A. Fleishman, George Mason University
Series Editor

CONTEMPORARY CAREER DEVELOPMENT ISSUES

Edited by

Robert F. Morrison
*Navy Personnel Research
and Development Center,
San Diego, California*

Jerome Adams
*Space & Defense Sector, TRW,
Redondo Beach, California*

LEA

LAWRENCE ERLBAUM ASSOCIATES, PUBLISHERS

1991   Hillsdale, New Jersey   Hove and London

Lawrence Erlbaum Associates, Inc., Publishers
365 Broadway
Hillsdale, New Jersey 07642

Library of Congress Cataloging-in-Publication Data

Contemporary career development issues / edited by Robert F. Morrison,
  Jerome Adams.
     p. cm. — (Series in applied psychology)
    Includes bibliographical references and index.
    ISBN 0-8058-0945-7
    1. Career development. I. Morrison, Robert F. II. Adams, Jerome. III. Series.
  HF5549.5.C35C66 1991
  658.3'142—dc20   90-20244
                                                        CIP

Printed in the United States of America
10 9 8 7 6 5 4 3 2 1

To *Anne Morrison* and *Debbie Adams*

Contents

About the Authors

Robert F. Morrison is in private practice as a consultant and a senior scientist at the Navy Personnel Research and Development Center. He has been on the faculties of the University of Toronto and West Virginia University. He has also held human resource management and personnel research positions with the Sun Company, Martin Marietta, The Mead Corporation, and Mobil Oil Company. He is the principal author of *Career Development for Engineers and Scientists* and the author of many articles and book chapters. He is a recipient of the American Psychological Association's James McKeen Cattell Award (now called the Ghiselli Award) for research design. His research, management, and consulting activities have dealt with career development, succession planning, and selection for scientists, professionals, and managers. He received his PhD in industrial psychology from Purdue University and MS and BS degrees from Iowa State University.

Jerome Adams is director of the Center for Leadership and Management Development for TRW's Space & Defense business. Prior to this position, he was at General Electric's Management Development Institute, "Crotonville," and a research professor of psychology and leadership at the United States Military Academy. He has authored and co-authored several books, monographs, and chapters including *Effective Leadership for Women and Men* and *Career Issues in Large, Complex Organizations*. He has published many articles on sex roles, leadership, and career issues in organizations. He is associate editor for the journal, *Military Psychology,* an editorial board member of the *Journal of Managerial Issues*, and a Fellow of the American Psychological Association. He earned a PhD from Purdue University, an MS from George Washington University, and a BA from Morgan State College.

Rabi S. Bhagat is professor of management in the Fogelman College of Business, Memphis State University and directs the doctoral program in organizational behavior. Previously, he was on the faculty of The University of Texas at Dallas. He is the author of numerous articles on organizational stress and cross-cultural management and a recipient of the American Psychological Association's James McKeen Cattell Award (now called the Ghiselli Award) for research design. He received his PhD from the University of Illinois in Urbana.

H. Dudley Dewhirst is professor of management and director of the Strategic Management Program at the University of Tennessee. Previously he was employed by Exxon in a variety of engineering and management positions. He has published extensively on the management of technical professionals. His research interests include information flows, leadership style, and the impact of organizational culture and systems on technical professionals. He holds a BS from Virginia Polytechnic Institute, an MBA from Harvard University, and a PhD from the University of Texas.

David L. Ford, Jr. is professor of organizational behavior in the School of Management at The University of Texas at Dallas. He has been on the faculty at Purdue University, a visiting professor at Michigan State and Yale Universities, and a visiting

ix

research scholar at UCLA. He has authored a book, *Readings in Minority Group Relations*, and a number of articles. He is chair of the Board of Directors of NTL Institute for Applied Behavioral Science and has served on the Editorial Board of the *Academy of Management Review*. His research interests include managing job stress and career development issues of female and dual career military officers. He received his PhD in organizational analysis from the University of Wisconsin-Madison.

Douglas T. (Tim) Hall is professor of organizational behavior and associate dean for faculty development, as well as a core faculty member of the Human Resources Policy Institute in the School of Management at Boston University. He has held faculty positions at Yale, York, Michigan State, and Northwestern Universities. At Northwestern he held the Earl Dean Howard Chair in Organizational Behavior and served a term as department chairman. He is the author of *Careers in Organizations* and co-author of *Organizational Climates and Careers, The Two-Career Couple, Experiences in Management and Organizational Behavior, Career Development in Organizations, Human Resource Management: Strategy, Design, and Implementation,* and *Handbook of Career Theory*. He is a recipient of the American Psychological Association's James McKeen Cattell Award (now called the Ghiselli Award) for research design. He is a Fellow of the American Psychological Association and of the Academy of Management, where he served on the Board of Governors. He has served on the editorial boards of five scholarly journals. His research and consulting activities have dealt with career development, women's careers, career burnout, two-career couples, and executive succession. He received his BS degree from Yale University and his MS and PhD degrees from Sloan School of Management at MIT.

Nancy Hicks is in private practice in Metuchen, New Jersey. She received her PsyD in clinical psychology from the Graduate School of Applied and Professional Psychology at Rutgers University.

Manuel London is professor and director of the Center for Labor/Management Studies in the Harriman School for Management and Policy, State University of New York at Stony Brook. Prior to joining Stony Brook, London worked for AT&T in a series of human resources and training positions. His books include *Developing Managers, Managing Careers, Career Management and Survival in the Work Place,* and *Managing the Training Enterprise*. He has been consulting editor for the *Academy of Management Journal* and currently serves on the editorial boards of *Personnel Psychology* and the *Journal of Applied Psychology*. His research interests include career development, personnel decisions, human resource forecasting and planning, and the human resources professional as a change agent. He received his PhD in industrial and organizational psychology from the Ohio State University.

Frank J. Minor is associate professor of Human Resource Management in the Department of Economics and Business Administration, Saint Anselm College, Manchester, New Hampshire. Prior to joining Saint Anselm, Minor was an associate professor at Northeastern University. Before joining Northeastern, he worked for IBM in a series of human resource management positions. His research has been published in applied psychology and human factors engineering journals, and he has been a contributing author to books. Minor has developed several computer-based systems to support employee and student career planning in corporations and high schools. He received a PhD in industrial psychology from the Ohio State University.

Roger A. Myers is professor of psychology and education at Teachers College, Columbia University where he teaches in counseling and organizational psychology programs. While at Teachers College, he has been director of the psychology division, chair of the Department of Psychology, and director of the doctoral programs in counseling and personnel psychology. He is co-author of *Counseling From Profiles*, an editor of *Behavior Change*, and co-author of two tests, the *Career Development Inventory* and the *Career Concerns Inventory*. He has been consulting editor for the *Journal of Counseling Psychology* and the *Academy of Management Executive*. He received his PhD in counseling psychology from the Ohio State University.

L. Allen Slade is an employee relations associate in the Employee Development Office of Ford Motor Company. Previously he was on the faculty at the University of Delaware. He is the author of several articles in scholarly journals. His research interests include career transitions, career counseling, assessment centers, managerial skills, and achievement motivation. He received his PhD in industrial and organizational psychology from the University of Tennessee.

Series Foreword

There is a compelling need for innovative approaches to the solution of many pressing problems involving human relationships in today's society. Such approaches are more likely to be successful when they are based on sound research and applications. This *Series in Applied Psychology* offers publications that emphasize state-of-the-art research and its application to important issues of human behavior in a variety of societal settings. The objective is to bridge both academic and applied interests.

Twenty years ago, there was little career development theory, even less research, and probably no applications beyond traditional training and management development that fell within the adult-life context. With a nagging feeling that adult life was not just a plateau in which a career decision made in late adolescence or early adulthood was played out until retirement, Robert Morrison left the industrial world of human resources management. He soon became embroiled in activities designed to satisfy his curiosity about how adults grow and develop throughout their life-long careers. Because of his experience with industry's leadership problems, foreign subsidiaries, organization start-ups, mergers and acquisitions, minority issues, and so on, he felt that the context within which an individual worked throughout an entire career strongly influenced the continuity of the growth and development process in concert with the individual's personal factors. His research has focused on these reciprocal concerns in career development.

Operating on a parallel path for more than 15 years, Jerome Adams has been a "student" trying to understand better the organizational career management and individual career development issues. The beginnings of that "student" learning journey involved work within the public sector where he observed and studied the changing values toward career success. Individuals were benchmarking career success and being influenced by new values: dual careers, heightened sense of work and family, and the general health and balance of quality of life. As the journey led to new opportunities involving work in the private section, the student was a witness to the new turbulence taking place in the business environment. Global competitiveness ushered in delayering, mergers, acquisitions, and the accelerated rate of change that redefined the importance of careful career management and creative career development. Over that 15-year journey, he has come to the realization that the successful linking of our research understanding of career issues with effective management practice provides a competitive advantage for the surviving organizations in the 1990s.

Morrison and Adams have both worked in and taught leadership, management, psychology, and human resource management over the last 30 years from their combined research and applied perspectives. They have bridged the two approaches by emphasizing the translation of theory into the applied world and the contribution of application to theory development. Adult career development has had a compelling and continuing attraction for both of them. This has been amply manifested during the last 15 years in the multimillion dollar, longitudinal research programs they have conducted independently in their respective military services, the U.S. Navy and the U.S. Army.

During the conduct of their research, they met and started contrasting their experience, results, and concerns. Then they decided to bring together senior human resource representatives of all major military services, industry practitioners from large, multinational companies, and noted scholars on career development issues from academia to look at the major gaps in officer career development that required research. Their thinking, and that of the major participants in the resulting workshop, formed the framework for this book. The material should serve as a stimulus for the reader to consider the long-range nature of career development and the importance to the organization of providing an appropriate context that supports individual career growth and development.

Edwin A. Fleishman, Editor
Series in Applied Psychology

Preface

Contemporary Career Development Issues is addressed to the human resource development specialists that desire to keep themselves and their programs current with contemporary issues and practices. The design of this book is based on the thesis that individuals develop, not in isolation but in a direction consistent with both personal needs and the needs of the surrounding environment. We have concentrated on the development of adults in their careers within an organization. Therefore, both organizational (career management) and individual (career planning) perspectives are included to present major elements in an organizational career development program.

Our aim is to provide practical guidance and examples for human resource development specialists to use in the evaluation of their current career development programs and the design of new ones. The topics covered in the text arose during a Tri-Service Career Research Workshop involving military and industry human resource management executives and the authors of the various chapters. Each chapter focuses on a key issue of today and extends it into the future by concentrating on present and potential applications. The original outline for each chapter was to start with a summary of relevant theory and current research on the topic. That introduction was to be followed by descriptions of applications that had demonstrated effectiveness, had failed in the past, or were showing promise at the present time. This was to be wrapped up in a summary that described future requirements for innovation, theory, and research. Although some of the topics are supported by theory and research, others are not, because the issues are not included in contemporary theory or research. An appropriate secondary use of this book would be as a supplemental text in a human resource management course at the advanced undergraduate or introductory graduate level in a university.

Because a program is effective in one organization does not mean that it would be effective in another. Where available, theory and research are described to aid human resource development managers in the design of new or modifications to present career development programs that function optimally in their specific organizations with their unique circumstances and requirements.

No effective organizational career development issue is totally an organizational or an individual concern; the two must interact. However, most programs are designed with either an organizational or an individual concern as primary. The book is organized to provide a flow for the reader from a key macro-organizational issue in chapter 2 to a principal micro-individual concern in chapter 6. To aid the reader to use the book as a reference for specific program design issues, the introduction (chapter 1) provides a summary of each chapter and points out specific questions the chapter can provide answers to.

How the organization strategy and the career development system strategy interact is described in chapter 2. The career development system can not remain viable and achieve its purposes unless it provides input to the organization's strategic planning and serves as an operational extension of that strategic plan. In this chapter, instances are summarized in which a specific organization strategy eliminates any need for a career development system while well-designed career development systems can contribute significantly to implementing other organization strategies.

The designers and managers of career development systems often overlook the fact that their programs will not work as desired unless the organizations' reward systems are consistent with the career development systems. As brought out in chapter 3, individual participation in career development system activities and outcomes must be rewarded and not punished or the purpose of the career development system will not be achieved. Each point of conflict between the reward system and the career development system will detract from optimizing achievement of the career development system goals.

The last macro, organizational chapter (chapter 4) focuses on career structural design concerns that are often overlooked. This chapter compares the unique characteristics of a growing population of professionals and semi-professionals with the career structures used to manage the developing careers of managers. Special issues, such as specialization, obsolescence, and the transition from specialist to manager, are reviewed in a career development system context.

Career transitions, an issue that is just starting to become a factor in career development system design and activities, are introduced in chapter 5. This chapter shifts the spotlight from a principal emphasis on the organization to one with a somewhat greater concentration on the individual. The individual's career transition process with each career change such as promotion, transfer, and new technology introduction is outlined, and organization programs, such as skills training and job previews, that can aid with transition adaptation are reviewed.

The individuals and their career decision making are emphasized in chapter 6. How people make career decisions and the factors affecting their decision processes form the introductory part of the chapter. Then the authors concentrate on actions that people and organizations take to help them make career decisions.

Although each chapter brings out what has been researched and which practices appear to be effective or ineffective, chapter 7 points out specific voids in our knowledge of career development that need to be filled in by research. Chapter 7 highlights five critical areas of knowledge, technology, and practice that need attention. These are mobility, strategic planning in career management, integrating career management and career planning, individual career transitions, and assessing the value of career development systems.

Preparing this book has been aided by so many colleagues and friends that they are too numerous to mention. They provided valuable anecdotes, practices, and insights. Special thanks goes to RADMs A. Herberger and R. Ustick who supported the Tri-Service Career Research Workshop with their time, ideas, and effort.

We hope that this volume proves to be a rich source of ideas for all who read it. Although it cannot provide a simple "cookbook" response to every specific problem, it can serve as a ready reference when learning about career development or designing a career development program or system.

Robert F. Morrison
Jerome Adams

1

Issues in the Management of Careers

Jerome Adams
Space & Defense Sector, TRW

> *To not invest in career planning and career development of managers is equivalent to planning to go out of business.*

The purpose of this book is to establish a link between those who study career issues and career development and those who are responsible for managing career programs in large, complex organizations. To achieve this goal, it is important to recognize that the nature and degree of interest in this topic varies considerably for members of each of these two groups. On the one hand, researchers and scholars may attempt to make important contributions to the general knowledge by emphasizing theory and empirical study. Alternatively, decision makers and policy formulators are frequently more practically oriented and seek answers about what to do, or what to implement, regardless of the availability (or existence) of supporting theory.

Consistent with the foregoing, this book focuses on three principal areas of concern: theory, research, and practice. Furthermore, an effective understanding of the career area requires strength in each area. Good theory is needed to foster sound research; sound research is needed to enhance theory; both are instrumental to the development of sound practice. The book itself is divided into seven chapters. To provide the reader with the appropriate frame of reference, this chapter focuses on defining key terms such as *career, career development, career planning,* and *career management.* Next, organization, or macrolevel concerns related to career management are discussed.

In succeeding chapters, the focus of each section becomes increasingly individual, or "micro," in orientation until the completion of chapter 6, dealing with career planning and decision making. The final chapter deals with summary statements regarding each of the three focal areas of concern. Because of this organizational flow, each chapter necessarily links to subsequent portions of the book. Occasionally, the reader will feel that topics overlap to some degree. When such overlap occurs, it is intentional because of the need to stress integration between what are often viewed as disparate areas within the career literature. Also, the reader is cautioned to keep in mind that what might appear to be the same program to some may in fact elicit quite a different viewpoint, dependent on the perspective of the viewer. For example, becoming plateaued in a work situation usually means quite different things when evaluated by policy planners in the affected organization or by the individual involved. In Peter's (1988) bestseller, *Thriving on Chaos*, he described a turbulent competitive environment of work. The 20 biggest deals of 1989, reported in *The Wall Street Journal* (Hilder, 1990), show that leverage-buy-outs and organizational restructuring have radically changed careers. To the organization a "downsized" work force is leaner, healthier— to the individual the situation means loss of promotion opportunity, less certainty about job security, all independent of his or her actual work performance.

Chapter 1 begins the introduction of careers in organizations by discussing some key terms. It becomes readily apparent that the study of careers has benefited from multiple theoretic approaches, but nothing close to a definitive statement has yet been made. However, by tying managerial careers to the concept of "choice," insights regarding the process of career development and behaviors encountered at different career stages are obtained. Furthermore, an accurate understanding of such insights is essential for those charged with developing policies and implementing career management decisions. In particular, the study of careers in the Department of Defense (DOD) is currently of great interest, both to the individual officers who serve in the various branches of the armed forces and to those in the DOD hierarchy who must develop policies and institute practices that govern and guide career development. A workshop was orchestrated at which leading academians and private industry practitioners came together with Army, Navy, and Air Force personnel and career managers to understand better career issues. Such interest intensifies with the realization that forces relating to statute and law (e.g., promotion policies, total force strength) often intervene to make certain career "choices" more attractive to the individual, but at the expense of total organization effectiveness. Because of the enormity and complexity of this problem, we should establish early what is meant by the term *career*.

THEORETICAL DEFINITIONS

Since the 1960s, much has been written about the topic of careers in organizations, resulting in numerous definitions of the term *career*. Unfortunately, however, no universally accepted definition has emerged from these many years of study. Several definitions to the notion of career are presented in this chapter, each reflecting, or emphasizing, a somewhat different aspect of a total definition. Given the focus of this book, each definition included has as its theme a theoretical connection to the process of career development.

Four basic definitions for the term *career* have been advanced, each thought to contribute uniquely to a comprehensive understanding, and each generally accepted (Hall, 1976). The first of these establishes the importance of "career as advancement." More specifically, a career represents a sequence of promotions and other moves in a work-related hierarchy during the course of a person's work life. Noteworthy in this aspect of the definition is the recognition that advancement can include lateral assignment to positions of enhanced responsibility or visibility within a particular organizational setting as well as moves to either better locations or organizations.

At the heart of this aspect of a definition of career is the assumption that upward mobility occupies a central position in what constitutes career success (Hall, 1976). In short, most of us place some value on advancement. Up is good; becoming plateaued or downward movement were generally viewed with disfavor. Within the military, where assignments and reassignments are written and published as "orders," and all recognition tied to advancement (e.g., promotions, selection for training awards, command selection) are published for all members of the organization to view, career advancement can readily be measured in terms of real or potential for upward mobility. Such an emphasis is not singularly restricted to the military establishment; many large corporations regularly publish the names of individuals who have met the requirements for advancement in position. At General Electric, persons selected to attend the month-long management programs at the internal institute, fondly called "Crotonville," signal that the majority of the participants have been screened and coded for "hi-pot" advancement in the organization (Adams, 1989a). Although these publications are explicitly designed to provide reward through recognition for achievement and potential, they also help to promote the concept of upward mobility. This particular topic is developed more fully in chapters 2 and 4 from both primarily organizational and individual vantage points.

Second, careers are also viewed as tied to a profession. Certain occupants have a built-in advancement potential, others do not. Jobs within occupational groupings that do not generally lead to advancement or to a long-term series of related positions are frequently viewed as not constituting a career.

This type of "professional" orientation to a definition of career includes an important criterion for success in that regular movements from one status to another within an occupational category frequently occur and that members of the occupation understand the pattern (Hall, 1976). This orientation is particularly appropriate in the military services where members openly display symbols designed to identify specific paths associated with career movement (e.g., aviator wings, submarine and surface warfare devices, green leadership tabs), although not necessarily restricted to military organization (e.g., airlines, police and fire departments). This aspect of the career definition is expanded more fully in chapter 4.

Third, a career is frequently viewed as a lifelong sequence of jobs. All people who work acquire work histories, and thus have careers. It is particularly important to note that no value judgment is made about either the type of occupation or the direction of movement that occurs. In this context, career is a more neutral, less value-laden term. Clearly, adherents to this aspect of the career definition value highly individual perceptions of the career rather than organizational expectations. Most agree that careers consist of at least two, separate parts. The first component is associated with the person's sequence of jobs which, in sum, constitute the objective career. Equally important, however, are individual evaluations and perceptions regarding how those objective work assignments combine to produce one's subjective career (Berlew & Hall, 1966; Hall, 1976). In chapter 6, concepts and issues related to career planning and decision making address this individual process more fully.

Finally, careers have been described as lifelong sequences of role-related experiences. Against this highly subjective standard, careers are viewed as individual representations of personal experiences within the job sequences referred to earlier. More specifically, the individual's perceptions of job activities, and the accompanying changes in aspirations, satisfaction, and self-concept derived from work and nonwork areas of a person's life contribute to this aspect of the definition. From this rather broad position, it is possible to view careers as a life process (Hall, 1976), which also incorporates as part of the process, aspects of involvement outside of work—roles that occupy significant amounts of time for most people (e.g., spouse, parent, community leader).

Each role can apply to a person regardless of either status or compensation. Within the Army, attention recently focused on demonstrating senior military leaders' concern for the special problems associated with family roles in military life. With the U.S. Army, there is a pre-command course to prepare leaders for battalion and brigade-level responsibilities. This organization also recognizes the role strain that command places on spouses. Thus, they have included spouses in a pre-command program. At General Electric, the executive education program designed for general managers had a spouse component module to raise the issues of family roles and ethical values (Adams, 1989a). The advent of the Navy's Family Service Centers are similarly associated with increased awareness of multiple roles that individuals must fill, and the conflict that frequently evolves from those competing role requirements. The final chapter of this book develops this theme more fully by identifying future research needs.

It should be clear that the four conceptual definitions presented here do not go together "hand-in-glove." Each perspective weighs differently some important aspect of work: the objective pattern of the career, the subjective experiences and judgments of individuals in response to objective patterns, and most globally, how a career might be extended beyond the scope of work alone to include almost any social category. Obviously, the concept of a career has meaning to both the individual job holders who are in pursuit of their careers, as well as to policymakers within the organizations human resource hierarchy who create developmental career paths for job holders to follow throughout their work lives. Less obvious, and in some ways more important, is our understanding of how and where individual and organizational career perceptions and expectations overlap, and the implications such overlap has for both individual and organizational effectiveness.

From the dichotomies contrasted in Table 1.1 it is easy to see that views on careers are likely different, dependent on vantage point. In addition, the extent to which any given individual will likely identify with one extreme or

TABLE 1.1
Organizational and Individual Perspectives
on Common Career Concepts

Organization Perspective	Individual Perspective
• Career based on advancement	• Career may or may not imply advancement
• Advancement has a prescribed path	• Advancement path may not be prescribed
• Little weight accorded to subjective experiences	• Heavy weight assigned to subjective experiences
• Value judgments are made about the type of job or job family	• Value judgments are made about the "type of job or the work itself
• Incentives are tied exclusively to organizational values	• Individuals increasingly question the organization's incentive package
• Success is based on an objective career sequence	• Success is more individually defined
• Institutional identity is cultivated	• Identity tied to specific activity or career field

another of any posted contrasts requires additional information concerning career stage and development. Thus, to foster positive career development within the military, or any large organization, requires a focus on the interaction between the individual and the referent organization throughout the career. The content of the interaction should change as different career issues become relevant at different points in the career.

INDIVIDUAL–ORGANIZATION CAREER INTERACTIONS

To best understand the interaction between the individual and the organization regarding the career, several different elements must be understood and viewed together (Schein, 1978). In a global sense, the individual and the organization exist within a society or culture that contribute to definitions of occupations, criteria for success, and expected or normative paths through life. In addition, culture, through its value system, influences the organization and the individual in more discrete ways as well. For example, statements regarding what is considered a good career, appropriate work, a good place to work, or an appropriate level of ambition in a given situation are frequently influenced by cultural values. For example, within the cultures of the Western industrialized world, working as a physician or surgeon excepting arguably obstetrics, would be valued as a good career affording status, financial rewards, and strong sense of self-worth. However, within the Soviet Union, the majority of physicians are women and the pay and status rewards are not valued as greatly as in the West. It will be interesting to see if the changing geopolitical situation in the Eastern block will change this cultural value. In essence, our cultural value system strongly affects our shared (i.e., individual and organizational) definition of career success.

Adopting this developmental perspective is not without problems. One of the dilemmas that immediately surfaces is that although the values surrounding definitions of work and a career are changing, the human resources hierarchy in most large organizations employ static values that are assumed to be valid among all organizational members. In the military services in particular, both organizations and individuals are influenced directly through various personnel policies and regulations, incentives (e.g., command assignments which enhance promotion opportunities), and through disincentives (e.g., remote assignments, frequent deployments). The intrusiveness of such influences suggests the need for congruence between system needs, career policies, and individual member needs. Because the career needs of its members do in fact change in response to changed social values, the military services must be prepared to take new and different steps where personnel policies are considered. For example, the individual at work, regardless of organizational referent, typically attends to occupational and educational opportunities, balancing career concerns with increasingly important concerns for family, self-development, and a lifestyle that has long-range viability. As more women enter the work force as full-time employees, both husbands and wives will be required to give increasing attention to managing "dual-career" families (Adams, 1985a, 1985b; Adams & Prince, 1984; Rapoport & Rapoport, (1985).

Schein (1978) noted that as individuals become affected, so must organizations. Unfortunately, there is no set of "matching processes" that brings the individual and the organization together ideally, into what should be a mutually profitable relationship. Recruitment, selection, training, job assignment, performance appraisal, and promotion would be better viewed as matching processes, not processes or events that are solely the prerogative of the organization in fulfilling its own needs. Thus, a recurring theme throughout this volume is that the way in which such human resource activities are in fact managed will strongly influence the long-range commitment by the individual to the parent organization. Additionally, effective career management will also directly influence, or limit, how viable and competitive an organization can be in competing for talented human resources. These two points are mutually dependent. For the long-term health of both their organization and the individual employee, leaders cannot ignore the consequences of how they manage careers of their people.

If Schein's (1978) concept of matching processes works well, both the organization and the individual will benefit. At the organizational level, increased creativity, productivity, and long-range effectiveness would likely be realized, whereas improved job satisfaction, personal development, and optimal integration of work and nonwork roles would be experienced by the individual. It is important to emphasize at the outset of this discussion that initial attempts at such organization planning must occur for the sake of increased organization effectiveness, regardless of the presence of individual-career planning activities (Schein, 1978). Far too often career planning ventures have been focused at the individual level, consisting largely of efforts provided to individuals. Unless equal or greater attention is paid to human resource planning and the extension of succession planning below executive levels as a major and essential organizational activity, fragmentation could result.

WHAT LIES AHEAD: AN OVERVIEW
OF THE CHAPTER CONTENTS

At the outset, the reader is reminded that the remainder of the book proceeds from a decidedly macro, nonindividualistic viewpoint to an increasingly individual perspective.

Chapter 2

This section provides a description and discussion of the area of career development and its relation to the organization's strategy. In this chapter, the perspective adopted is that of the organization and how the career development system should adopt to reflect the realities of its long-range strategy. Therefore, relevant topics include the organization's career management policy and programs involving such issues as manpower planning, the assessment of performance (and potential), succession planning, education, training, management development, and career planning systems.

The increase in the attention provided the concept of career management at the level of the organization over the last few years has been impressive. Until most recently, writings and guidelines on career programs have been for the most part tailored to individual planning and decision making. The reason for this internally focused, somewhat personal emphasis seems to be associated with an apparent lack of concern for a number of "external" or "environmental context" factors that now are seen as affecting an organization's career management system. Within the military services, for example, issues like manpower planning, education and training, and appraisal and assessment almost totally ignored the exigencies outside of the Armed Forces. In 1973, the advent of the All Volunteer Force quickly changed that staid philosophy; the seemingly unlimited pool of manpower resource ended with the termination of the draft.

In response to this change, the military was forced to compete in the "market place" more vigorously for its managerial (i.e., officer) talent. As an organization, the Department of Defense attempted to secularize its manpower-based marketing strategy. This shift was seen as movement away from a career primarily based on an institutional orientation (self-sacrifice and dedication to sense of duty as a calling) toward more of an occupational orientation characterized by self-interest and marketplace values (Moskos, 1977). The end result of this process is that many members now view their military service not as a "career," but rather as just another job.

Viewed from a somewhat different vantage point, the military's interest in career management lies in producing enough trained and experienced officers to fill positions in response to national security needs that define the Armed Forces role to the national strategy. Simply stated, the military and its systems aim to produce officers capable of handling current and projected responsibilities when and where they are required. However, individual interests are increasingly self-directed. Although the military, or other large organizations, may need a new set of skills to respond to rapid technological changes in equipment, individuals may be unwilling to acquire them.

The reasons that exist in support of an organizational emphasis on career management are too numerous to mention (Dewhirst, 1984). Armed service needs may require large numbers of officers to be in certain places for many of the individuals involved. Any organization's mission or function may require complete and absolute concentration and dedication from the individual at a time when the employee is experiencing the stress of personal crisis. When natural or environmental disasters occur (e.g., hurricanes, earthquakes, tanker spills, oil platform fires, etc.,) or sanitization demands that individuals are on hand even if there is a serious domestic problem in the individual's life. Obviously the differences are many, and center on career responsibilities and organizational needs on one hand and very personal, perhaps idiosyncratic, individual set of needs on the other. In short, organizationally oriented career management systems in large organizations must effectively seek to fill their mission needs and concomitantly be aware that individuals are increasingly evaluating overall life experiences in terms of work and nonwork factors.

These and other topics provide the gist of chapter 2. In more detail, the discussion of career management issues revolves around the following seven questions:

1. **What factors should be considered in strategic planning at the corporate/organization and business/mission levels that are important in career development?**
2. **How can the linkage between strategic planning of the organization, human resource management, and career development levels be made?**
3. **What functions are relevant to the career management and career planning subsystems of a career development system?**
4. **What assumptions and requirements are key to an effective career development strategy and system?**
5. **What corporate/organization strategies make career development inappropriate or not feasible?**
6. **What career development programs are most applicable to different business strategies?**
7. **What are some good and bad examples of career development systems and how can their ability to influence and contribute to business strategy be improved?**

Chapter 3

Like chapter 2, chapter 3 is primarily organizational in its focus but contributes to the integration of the individual's career planning and development within the context of the organization's career management system. The central issue in this chapter is focused on the organization's reward system and how it influences the behavior and career development of its human resources. More specifically, this chapter addresses the problem of incentives, disincentives, and barriers to career development.

In many organizations, the compensation system is considered the only formal reward system. However, in career development the promotion policies and practices (e.g., up or out) and the attractiveness of organizational subunits, specific jobs or projects, and locations are less tangible, but viable elements in the reward system. Inconsistent or unequal career requirements or opportunities, poor management support, preferences that are not considered, and punishments for career behaviors/assignments (e.g., out-of-sight, out-of-mind in a foreign job) form barriers to obtaining the available rewards.

Since the 1980s, there has been a growing recognition that the values surrounding success in work are changing. One would be hard pressed to suggest that traditional work-related values have remained stable. For example, the emergence of the women's movement has come as a strong challenge to the institutionalized division of labor between the sexes. The continuing generation-related value shifts still has children of the middle class rebelling against the traditional American success syndrome of climbing the socioeconomic ladder. Finally, there has been a gradual turning away from the view that work must necessarily be a source of primary life satisfaction (Schein, 1967, 1978). For instance, the requirements of a work career no longer are assumed to take precedence automatically in a man's life, nor are they presumed, pro forma, to be secondary in a woman's life These issues become even more complex given the demographic changes projected for the work force by the year 2000.

An obvious conclusion drawn from the foregoing statements is that the success ethic is changing (Hall, 1976). In the past, success was most likely to be defined in terms of external factors such as salary, position level, or status. Now there is a greater tendency for people to employ a personal criterion for success, usually with an emphasis or focus on self-fulfillment and happiness. The implications for the military services and other large organizations are straightforward. If the research conducted to date is accurate, the shift in definitions of success from traditional to personal will mean a decrease in emphasis on performance indicators and increased emphasis on career attitudes, such as satisfaction and commitment, and psychological well-being. Accompanying the increased emphasis on individual notions of success is the suggestion of less organizational control of its members and the requirement to reexamine the types of incentives offered to employees.

A general framework for understanding career incentives and disincentives must describe the "incentive/disincentive package" from two separate, but interacting perspectives: (a) the reward incentive structure as defined by the organization, which involves policies and expectations about which employees will move into what positions and how quickly; and (b) the expectations and values of the employees who must move through the organization's career patterns.

It is important to realize that any description of the reward and incentive structure in an organization must include both tangible and intangible rewards. For example, compensation in the military includes Congressionally regulated pay and allowances as well as intrinsic compensation such as awards, decorations, citations, and so on. Although promotions might very well represent the best organizational incentive, increase in rank typically affords the incumbent the chance to exercise power, experience greater amounts of autonomy, challenging work or assignments, and acquire greater status or prestige. Organizational incentives such as these fit well the "career as advancement" orientation described earlier.

On the other hand, individual expectations are not always fully aligned with the organization's reward structure. Some reasons why there may be a mismatch between the organization's incentive and reward structure and personal values include low levels of challenge in initial job assignments, unrealistically high aspirations on the part of the employee, and other such changes in individual expectation that may lead to the development of a career anchor. For example, in the aerospace business at General Electric, a career study of new college hires found that persons in aerospace were least satisfied, least challenged, and least likely to stay with General Electric after 5 years. A closer examination of the work given this well-paid, highly recruited group revealed that a 6- to 8-month delay in security clearance processing created a situation of giving them unclassified, peripheral low-level tasks. General Electric conducted focus group meetings to discuss the security process and the plan to update realistic preview in recruiting efforts to align better expectation with early job experience (Adams, 1989b).

Other topics discussed in chapter 3 include:

1. How effective are pay, compensation, and other extrinsic rewards in attracting and keeping highly qualified personnel in specific careers?

Are some rewards (or combinations thereof) more effective than others for certain types of individuals or career areas (e.g., early vs. late career, line vs. staff positions) in motivating performance? What constraints arise when relying on pay and other extrinsic rewards as career incentives?

2. In what ways does the initial job assignment impact one's subsequent career success?

How critical is initial assignment success or failure on career path progression for different types of careers (e.g., line vs. staff, generalist vs. specialist)? What problems exist in the way in which the initial job assignment serves as an incentive or disincentive for different career types or categories?

3. What problems need to be addressed in the design of specific jobs to make them more attractive?

Are job complexity and intrinsic motivation factors major concerns for certain career categories or anchors (linear, spiral, technical vs. managerial) as well as for certain career specialties (line vs. staff, generalist vs. specialist)? What are the key dimensions or characteristics of job attractiveness that are critical for military versus other careers (e.g., variety, feedback, etc.)?

4. What problems are caused by the inconsistent application of policies, job requirements, and career management systems across various career specialties?

How does career progression involving movement back and forth between different career specialties impact individuals at different career stages and what are those effects? Should continued promotion (upward movement) always be the determinant or definition of success and should organization exit be the only alternative for "failure?"

5. What problems are present in the amount and types of managerial support that is or is not provided to persons in various career specialties?

How much managerial support should be provided to different career specialties or to individuals at different career stages that would afford those people opportunity for visibility and exposure to different parts of the organization? What is the impact of that exposure and support on subsequent career success?

6. If career stage is measured in terms of time in the profession rather than as chronological age, what special problems/opportunities exist for individuals at later stages of a career?

Because career stage and chronological age often are not perfectly matched, what are the frustrations that would cause a person to retire at the earliest possible opportunity versus the incentives associated with retention beyond the early retirement point? Are such incentives different from those that prove effective at earlier career stages and are they likely to be more effective with certain career categories than others?

Chapter 4

Although many of the generic career management programs and policies introduced in chapter 2, as well as the incentives, disincentives, and barriers to career development identified in chapter 3 are important to our enhanced understanding of careers, their translation into action constitutes the real measure of success for any organization. Chapters 4 and 5 are concerned with issues affecting the translation process and specifically focus on (a) the basics of mobility, specialization, and their combined effects on the full course of a career; and (b) problems faced by organizations in facilitating individual effectiveness (e.g., technical obsolescence, management of plateaued employees).

In every career, a process occurs through which a person moves from being a learner to being a contributor. Such movement reflects one's skills that have become refined and honed during early career stages (Schein, 1978). Within the military, as with all organizations, regardless of whether the contribution is made as a pilot, computer software specialist, logistician, and so on, the early career period is the time when the job incumbent becomes very good at the job and subsequently makes a contribution through the application of highly developed skills. A major problem for the organization is the decision of whether a person's long-range contribution will hinge on the continued exercise of early skills (specialization), or whether the contribution will be maximized by the acquisition of more general, managerial skills. Frequently the consequence of the career pattern decision, once made, is irreversible. For example, after investing approximately $2 million to train and certify a pilot, the Navy and Air Force may be reluctant to allow changes to different career paths.

Several different patterns have been identified in the career literature cited and discussed in chapter 4. These include:

- *Traditional vertical* is where one enters an organization in a particular position and whatever mobility occurs is vertical. In small organizations, opportunities to advance depend heavily on changeover at the next higher level.
- *Trunk and branch,* as the name suggests, is a more elaborate pattern of career mobility that is best depicted by the trunk and branches of a tree. In this scheme, career patterns only begin as vertical (trunk) but provide multiple opportunities for "branching" into different functions or specialties. Each branch has its own line of progression and opportunities exist for further branching. Both individuals and organizations have greater flexibility.
- *Planned job rotation* introduces centralized control regarding job rotation. A supervisor (or organizational unit) is advised that an individual will be assigned to a work unit for a specified period of time, subsequent to additional job assignments. Mobility is typically lateral and vertical and provide breadth of experience to organization members.
- *Dual-ladder* systems offer, after some specified entry period, separate but parallel paths to vertical advancement. Mobility requires a choice between two different sets of skills and experiences and typically

includes a line or generalist base as well as a specialist or professional track. Once the choice is made, advancement occurs along a vertical career path.

- *Multiple career path* systems involve career assignments in a primary area that are interspersed with secondary jobs. Mobility is typically accomplished through a combination of vertical and lateral assignments. Throughout the course of a career, an employee may rotate between organizational specialty areas.

Each of the possible career patterns just described differs in terms of the advantages and limitations provided to personnel policymakers who must forecast human resource needs compatible with organizational requirements. As mentioned earlier, poorly made decisions could have irrevocable consequences. Within the military context, to begin in a warfare specialty is to enter a specific career ladder and to embark on a different sequence of jobs from those available to the technical specialist. These differences contribute greatly to determining individual effectiveness of organizational members, especially where issues regarding transitions from specialist to manager, technological obsolescence, and management of plateaued workers are of concern.

In this context, many organizational members unconsciously adopt unrealistic career goals or engage in ineffective behaviors consistent with the expectation that they will rise onward and upward forever (Ferrence, 1979; Ferrence, Stoner, & Warren, 1977). Are such ambitions those of the individual, or simply widely perceived organizational expectations? A conscious, thoughtful reappraisal of the realities and options, at both the individual and organizational level, will increase the likelihood of career satisfaction, at least in terms of what has been described as "psychological success." Whether such problems can be dealt with in terms of transitional processes, improved understanding of technological obsolescence, or increased awareness of the nature of career plateaus is discussed in the final portion of chapter 4 approached from organizational systems, work assignment/environment, and individual support perspectives.

Other topics discussed in chapter 4 address the following questions:

1. What problems are faced in determining and managing the relationship between successful specialized and generalized managerial careers?

How broad (or narrow) should the scope of various job assignments be over the course of a career? Do the identified advantages of specialized (or generalized) career paths depend on age or career stage categories? If so, how?

2. What problems are present in the amount of structure that is or is not provided concerning career paths?

Assuming that job assignments "A," "B," and "C" provide important experience for job assignment "D," should those earlier positions be made formal, prerequisites? How much opportunity should be designed into a system to allow individuals to modify, combine, or switch career tracks? If routes to the top are explicit, do the advantages of such a system outweigh the potential dysfunctional effects?

3. What problems exist in making multiple ladder and dual-ladder career path systems effective?

Which career system is superior? What are the organizational or environmental characteristics that facilitate the implementation of one approach versus another? Which is more likely effective in military settings?

4. What problems are likely to occur as a professional begins the transition from specialist to generalist?

What are the major differences in roles and what skills are important for success at each end of the transition continuum? Among the various aids to transition (e.g., training, coaching, short-term assignments), which are the most effective? Are the identified problems more or less pronounced in military settings than they are in industry?

5. What problems need to be resolved to insure the effective utilization and continuing motivation of the plateaued employee?

(Being plateaued is not intended to imply that performance is poor or has declined. It simply means that the individual affected cannot or will not be promoted, for any of several reasons.) How should plateaued workers be managed so as to maintain optimal and continued productivity. What barriers to the effective use of plateaued employees must be overcome? Are problems associated with plateaued employees of greater concern in military organizations?

6. In what ways is the obsolescence of technical knowledge, skill, or attitudes of employees a significant organizational problem?

What can be done to prevent or counter technological, managerial, or other kinds of obsolescence? How do we keep military officers more up to date as an attempt to slow down obsolescence?

Chapter 5

This section is concerned with career transitions and change, both topics seen as important given the increasing incidence in when jobs and professions have changed today. Such turnover places greater demands on the recruiting, training, and other human resource development programs of organizations in an attempt to attract and retain highly qualified professionals. It is important to note that at this point the individual is becoming more recognizable as the central unit in our discussion of careers. Organizations, at least in the next two chapters, are viewed as settings that individuals choose among as places to best play out the balance in both work and nonwork needs. Thus, this chapter becomes a mixture of both organizational and individual emphasis. The organization can provide the opportunity for individuals to make career transitions and to participate in programs that support people experiencing transitions. Although traditional emphasis has been on changing occupations, relocation, and improving socialization during initial organizational entry, recent attention has focused on other types of transitions (e.g., promotion, demotion, reassignment/job rotation) as well as the employee's adaptability and ability to cope with stress.

Several societal trends have contributed to the increasing prevalence of job and profession changing, as well as other types of career transitions noted earlier. There is now a broader concern with overall quality of life as contrasted with the more traditional (and narrower) definition of success and "climbing the corporate ladder." There was an increased emphasis during the 1960s and 1970s on personal growth and fulfillment, lifestyle experimentation, and individualism (Hall, 1976). Additionally, individuals have reexamined work and nonwork (e.g., family) priorities and now seemingly demand more from all life activities (Rapoport & Rapoport, 1969). Finally, there is a growing number of dual-career families, and correspondingly greater consideration is being given to their special needs (Levinson, Darrow, Klein, Levinson, & McKee, 1974; Rapoport & Rapoport, 1976).

Trends such as those just mentioned have led to a growth in the number of workers who undertake career transitions. As previously noted, transitions may result in a change of job or profession or a change in one's orientation to work while continuing in the same job. Associated with any career transition are personal and financial costs that accrue to the organizations involved, the individuals in transition, and their families. Therefore, it is increasingly important to understand and facilitate career transitions.

To begin with, a transition suggests both a change and a period during which the change is taking place (Louis, 1980). The central idea associated with the concept of career is the "role" (i.e., the task or other behaviors associated with a position in an organization or social system), and both subjective and objective aspects of roles are included. Therefore, we adopt the following definition: "Career transition is the period during which an individual is either changing roles (taking on a different objective role) or changing orientation to a role already held (altering a subjective state)."

There are several types of career transitions, including initial job entry, reassignment/job transfer, mid-life changing fields of work or occupation, and retirement. Correspondingly, there are two major categories of transitions: (a) interrole, where a new and different role is actually taken (e.g., a dentist who becomes a priest); (b) intrarole, which represents an adjustment in orientation to a role already held (e.g., a military officer experiencing and evaluating different issues, personal needs, and organizational opportunities associated with his or her career). Our discussion is limited to primarily interrole transitions because of the implications that increased understanding of this phenomenon has for the organization as a whole, as well as for the human resource specialist who must develop career plans. Furthermore, distinctions are made between those transitions that are associated with disruptive versus adaptive processes.

Within the military context, assignment planners are principally concerned with what happens to an officer during one of the various types of transitions (e.g., geographic relocation, job changes, plateauing, retirement). For example, when an officer enters a new assignment, usually accompanied by geographical relocation, there is a new role orientation to be adopted. Not unlike the case in private industry, the officer examines differences between the old and new role primarily in terms of (a) objective features of the job or assignment itself, (b) subjective or perceived shifts in job or organizational goals, and (c) discrepancies or departures from what is expected that inevitably occur. Coping with these differences represents an important issue during the transitioner's early experiences in the new setting.

Specific questions addressed in chapter 5 include:

1. What kinds of problems exist concerning the number of career transitions required by employees regarding their ability to contribute to organizational effectiveness?

How similar is the process of adapting to different types of transitions (i.e., promotion, new assignment, relocation, etc.) for different types of occupational/professional specialties? What should be done to facilitate the adaptation process?

2. How does the concept of employment security apply to careers?

If demotion is a reasonable policy, in what cases (and how) would it be implemented? What advantages and disadvantages are associated with providing employment security in the military? For example, the recent events of Eastern Europe cause a new examination in the role of NATO and the number of conventional soldiers in Europe. The discussions of group cutbacks create a new challenge in how to examine the concept of employment security—something in the private sector that has been underway since the early 1980s.

3. How serious are the problems of geographical relocation especially offshore and international assignments?

How could staffing and training programs be modified if there is a decrease in the willingness to relocate? What could be done to increase the willingness to relocate? What policies could be changed to (a) decrease the need for relocation, and (b) facilitate job and personal adjustment after relocation?

4. In what ways is plateauing a career transition problem?

How does structural plateauing (the perception that future promotions are unlikely) affect an officer's perception of his or her career? How does content plateauing (the perception that future changes in job content are unlikely) affect an individual's perceptions of his or her career? How can subordinates be better prepared for plateauing in a manner that could lead to better personnel management?

5. What should be the objectives of pre-retirement planning programs?

What, if anything, is wrong with current programs? How should the content of pre-retirement program be changed? How would an organization assess the quality and effectiveness of a newly designed, pre-retirement planning program? Golden handshakes are a by-product of leveraged buy-outs; restructuring and organizational downsizing are more the norm than the exception. Even "big blue" IBM hit recently by computer sales soft market and fierce competition has had three generous work release offer packages and very lucrative pre-early retirement programs.

6. What should senior executives do to enhance the career flexibility of their subordinates so they are familiar with their job and career options and can optimize their "transition" decisions?

What are the most serious deficiencies in trying to be flexible and adapting one's career to changing "business demands" (e.g., lack of information, inaccurate information, poor skills training, inadequate development planning process, nonexistent counseling services, etc.).

Chapter 6

In chapter 6, our focus shifts even further from more macro, organizational issues toward individual, career development issues. Of concern in this chapter is determining what the organization can provide in the way of career decision aids for its employee's career decision support systems. Additionally, typically effective and ineffective individual decision styles, training programs that might facilitate individual decision making, and extant programs designed to train supervisors in "career coaching" are identified.

Presently, however, no theories of career decision making exist that specifically address the individual working in an organizational setting. The lack of such theories presents a problem in that an organization can exercise considerable influence on what career choices the individual makes, how they are made, and what information is utilized in the process. As such, many career decisions are made based on discrepancies between individual preferences and perceived organizational needs. Some career decisions do not appear to arise as a result of such discrepancies. Instead, they are the response of a person to an opportunity presented by the organization to the individual (e.g., early retirement, early promotion).

The cognitive processes used by employees to arrive at their response to such situations may not be prospective or sequential in nature. Instead, employees may use retrospective and rationalizing processes as the basis to accept or reject opportunities. If this is the case, the individuals may not be as active participants in the development of their career paths as current vocational decision making models have hypothesized. Hence, the need to examined in some detail the career decision making process.

Factors Influencing Career Decisions. As indicated earlier, career decisions are initiated by the individual, by the organization, or by both. From the individual's perspective, the precipitant of the decision process can be either a perceived discrepancy or a presented opportunity. As is made evident in chapter 6, understanding this distinction is important. One of the most significant individual elements affecting career change may be the impact of life stages on career development, and correspondingly on career decision making. For example, the transition from early to middle adulthood can result in a period of crisis that becomes the impetus for a career decision (Levinson et al., 1974).

Nonwork variables also influence career decision making (London & Stumpf, 1982). Mobley (1982) cited both nonwork values and nonwork roles as important contributing factors to employee turnover. Nonwork roles include marital status, family members, parenthood, leisure interest, religious and altruistic commitments, and whether one is a member of a dual-career couple. Nonwork values are linked to nonwork roles, and reflect beliefs and preferences regarding lifestyle, geographic location, religious and cultural affiliations, family orientation, and social practices. The individuals who wish to remain close to their families or origin, or whose spouses and children prefer not to move, are less likely to accept a promotion to a new location than employees who are unmarried, not single-parents, and eager for novel experiences.

Finally, there are practical implications to career decision making, at least to the extent that we can apply our knowledge of basic decision processes to this area. For example, identifying the influence of the career decision would be beneficial for both the individual and the organization. The employee will learn how such things as the organization's policies, structure, and information availability influence the career decision. Policy planners and human resource specialists would be in a better position to support career decision making and planning by being cognizant of, and attentive to, individual needs at different career stages. Additionally, considerable effort could be expended in making employees more aware of legitimate discrepancies between their expectations and reality.

An example of how such an interaction has been structured and implemented exists in the U. S. Army. Military job assignments have traditionally been centrally managed by occupational specialty. For the most part, the personnel policy planner fills specific positions based on operational requirements. In the past, each member of a dual military career couple was required to communicate separately for job assignments, which led to considerable conflict. The Army now has a marital code that requires personnel assignment officers to consider both officers' needs for joint domicile as well as operational requirements. As a result, stimulating "good" decision making (e.g., decision based on accurate information) contributes to the vitality of the organization. Individuals who have adequately assessed both themselves and their environment before making a decision are likely to be most satisfied with their career choices. Finally, encouraging realistic career planning and providing accurate information early in a person's career highlights the value of the employee's contribution to the organization and, in time, may diminish the distance between expectations and organizational reality.

Other questions addressed in chapter 6 include:

1. What is the organizational impact on commitment?

How does the organization affect individuals' career decisions in ways that are likely to increase their level of commitment to the organization? For instance, choices that are made from among a number of alternatives, that are public, explicit, and irrevocable, are more apt to lead to commitment. Information salience can increase commitment, as can the organization's willingness to be responsive to the needs of its employees.

2. What is the value of enhancing the individual's contributions ?

When individuals feel their work is important and of value to the organization, they tend to be more satisfied and may decide to exert extra energy within their work roles. Employees do not always understand the value of their contributions. How can the importance of their contributions be demonstrated to them in such a way that it increases the likelihood of their remaining with the organization?

3. How important is maintaining the availability of accurate career information?

Information that is available to employees and that is perceived as relevant to their needs can have an effect upon whether they choose to stay with an organization. Either recruitment or retention may be impacted by information salience. How and when can information be used to highlight the attractiveness of organizational alternatives, as well as their relevance to the individual? How should career information be disseminated within the organization? Should this be integrated with a self-assessment process for employees? Should information about career opportunities both within and outside the organization be made available?

4. What is the impact of the nonwork situation on career decisions?

Looking at the whole person is an important part of career planning in the organizational context. What a person's nonwork roles and values are, and how the individual sees themselves are all issues the organization needs to address in providing employees with attractive career alternatives. How might a organization go about responding to individuals as whole persons?

5. What are the advantages to career choices and career pathing?

When individuals think they have had a choice in making a decision, they are likely to feel satisfied with the decision and to commit themselves to it. In terms of recruitment, for instance, how can individuals be offered a variety of alternatives from which they might choose a desired career option? How could this be done in mapping out employee career paths so as to encourage retention? What kinds of standard career paths and employee training programs should an organization offer its employees? How flexible should these be? By what process should they be evaluated and revised?

6. How useful are self-assessment, career planning programs?

Should an organization develop self-assessment career planning programs? If so, what form might they take? Should they involve the use of mini-computers? What about incorporating evaluations from supervisors and peers? What other training opportunities and career information should be offered in conjunction with such programs? Should there be an assessment center for skill and motivation identification?

7. What is the role of the supervisor?

Should an organization educate its managers and supervisors on career development issues and on reinforcing their subordinates on the value of career development? What kind of training should the supervisors receive? The challenges in the 1990s for first-level supervisors will be enormous. Worker spans of control have already grown from 7 to 10 more toward 18 to 20. The role of the supervisor according to Drucker (1988) resembles an orchestra conductor whose job is to bring harmony among many talented specialists.

Chapter 7

The final chapter reviews the various topics and ideas that represent the main body of the book and raises questions about the field of career development that must be addressed in the near future. The problem of mobility in a career, for example, is addressed because it is rich with both theoretical and practical concerns. Specific points developed in this discussion include relationships between mobility and performance, mobility and personal well-being, identification of employee career and family characteristics related to mobility effects, and differences in mobility rates associated with organization growth. Consistent with the book's focus on both individual and organizational approaches to the examination of career issues, a considerable portion of the final chapter examines organizational career systems and how they must be better designed to interact with individual level career concerns. Examples of topics addressed in this chapter include:

1. How can better integration between individual and career planning processes and organizational career management systems be obtained?

Although we are better able to deal with this question today than in the past, more emphasis must be placed in the area of strategic human resource planning and development. Organizations must adopt longer range views regarding changes in the composition of their work force so as to identify meaningful career paths for their employees. In this way the individual's career planning efforts can be more accurately matched with organizational opportunity.

2. Can we identify the positive and negative aspects associated with career mobility?

Of the many issues available for discussion, a special point of interest revolves around concerns over individual performance and productivity. For example, in a given job move situation (requiring a given amount of skill and psychological change), how does performance change over time, both before and after the job move? Are their corresponding productivity changes at the organizational level that can be measured if the organization's policy is to move many members on a frequent basis.

3. What are the organizational responses necessary to ensure continued proactive movement in career development that maximizes individual needs and organizational goals?

As discussed more completely in this concluding section, organizations need to become more aware of their employees' need for information during important points of interaction between the individual and the employer. Second, employees at all levels of the organization need to have nonpunitive opportunities to express their feelings about their careers. How the organization chooses to generate and implement policy in these areas and apply them to different classes of employees (e.g., "fast-trackers" vs. "steady-state workers" is of crucial importance of the development of effective career management systems.

Although each chapter not only brings out the state of our knowledge, what has been researched, and which practices appear to be effective, the acid test of value added for most organizations dealing with career development and management will be assessed by the degree that they are able, in the mid-1990s and beyond, to build viable careers for tomorrow's leaders.

REFERENCES

Adams, J. (1989a). *Corporate management education and development at General Electric.* Unpublished manuscript.

Adams, J. (1989b). *Early career perceptions of professional new hires at General Electric.* Unpublished manuscript.

Adams, J. (1985a). *Report of the early career preparation, experiences, adjustments, and commitment of male and female West Point Graduates.* West Point, NY: The AG Printing Office.

Adams, J. (1985b). *Longitudinal study of army officer careers.* West Point, NY: The AG Printing Office.

Adams, J., & Prince, H. T. (1984). *An investigation of the impact of work and family.* Paper presented at the Inter-University Seminar on Armed Forces and Society, Chicago, IL.

Berlew, E. E., & Hall, D. T. (1966). The socialization of managers. *Administrative Science Quarterly, 11,* 207–223.

Drucker, P. (1988). The coming of the new organization. *Harvard Business Review, 66,* 45–53.

Dewhirst, D. (1984). *Specialization, career patterns, and career structure.* Paper presented at the Tri-Service Conference on Career Development, San Diego, CA.

Ferrence, T. P. (1979). The career plateau: Facing up to life at the middle. In M. Jelinek (Ed.), *Career management for the individual and the organization* (pp. 175–180). Chicago: St. Clair Press.

Ferrence, T. P., Stoner J. A. F., & Warren, E. K. (1977). Managing the career plateau. *Academy of Management Review, 2* (4), 602–612.

Hall, D. T. (1976). *Careers in organizations.* Santa Monica, CA: Goodyear.

Hilder, D. B. (1990, January 2). The 20 biggest deals completed in 1989. *The Wall Street Journal,* p. 8.

Levinson, D. J., Darrow, C., Klein, E., Levinson, M., & McKee, B. (1974). The psychological development of man in early adulthood and mid-life transition. In D. F. Hicks, A. Thomas, & M. Roff (Eds.), *Life history research in psychopathology* (pp. 123–147). Minneapolis: University of Minnesota Press.

London, M., & Stumpf, S. (1982). *Managing careers.* Reading, MA: Addison-Wesley.

Louis, M. (1980). Career transitions: Varieties and commonalities. *Academy of Management Review, 5,* 329–340.

Mobley, W. H. (1982). *Employee turnover: Causes and consequences.* Reading, MA: Addison-Wesley.

Moskos, C. (1977). From institution to occupation: Trends in military organization. *Armed Forces and Society, 4,* 44–50.

Peters, T. (1988). *Thriving on chaos.* New York: Random House.

Rapoport, R., & Rapoport, R. N. (1969). The dual-career family: A variant pattern and social change. *Human Relations, 22,* 3–30.

Rapoport, R., & Rapoport, R. N. (1985). *Report to the officer corps: Results of the professional development of officers study surveys.* Washington, DC: Office of Public Affairs.

Schein, E. H. (1967). Attitude change during management education. *Administrative Science Quarterly, 11,* 601–628

Schein, E. H. (1978). *Career dynamics.* Reading, MA: Addison-Wesley.

2

Meshing Corporate and Career Development Strategies

Robert F. Morrison
Navy Personnel Research and Development Center

This chapter departs from the generic chapter outline that was described in chapter 1. A descriptive model of a career development system and its supporting programs is put forth with research support introduced in the sparse instances that it is available. Concurrently, major organizational practices are depicted as examples when they have (a) demonstrated effectiveness over an adequate period of time, (b) been based on careful analysis of the organization's needs and culture, or (c) represent an apparent foundation in sound theory or past experience. There is a developing area of research and theory about career development systems and their component subsystems but a dearth in two areas: How to link career development subsystems with human resource and corporate/business strategic plans and where career development subsystems work and do not work (T. Gutteridge, personal communication, April 13, 1990). This chapter should help fill that void as we move into an era that will require career development to demonstrate such linkage and the effectiveness of programs (Leibowitz & Forrer, 1990).

Because we cannot introduce the theory and research conducted in those two areas, provide examples of effective and ineffective practices, and summarize what needs to be done, an alternate approach would be to take the practices of various organizations and to treat them as though they were quasiexperimental designs of the simplest form. Effective system linkages and career development programs would be compared qualitatively via content analytical procedures with ineffective system linkages and programs considering the content of the career development system and programs, presence and content of supporting programs, and the situational contexts even though the system linkages and program loci were in different organizations. The criterion for an effective system/programs would be whether they continued in use within the organization for a finite period of time; possibly 5 years or more and met some specified organization requirement(s). We might assume that a system/program that was discontinued within such a time period was not contributing to the organization's requirements and, therefore, was no longer effective. By comparing systems/programs that were continued with those that were discontinued, we might be able to assess the systems/programs content and environment to establish a normative model of an effective career management system, its component programs, the supporting system/program requirements, and the environmental conditions that make them succeed or fail. The only problem with this alternate approach is that hardly any information is available. Organizations do not report carefully about unsuccessful system linkages and programs. In addition, organizations often exaggerate the effectiveness of programs that are presented or make a premature, optimistic assessment of results that should be evaluated after several years, not immediately. Establishing and conducting such a research design would be costly and time consuming but would make a major contribution to the field of career development when it is done. Until then, we will have to take advantage of what is acknowledged as the best of what is known. This chapter presents state-of-the-art information about how a career development system can be linked to the corporate/business strategy and which career development subsystems contribute significantly to alternative business strategies.

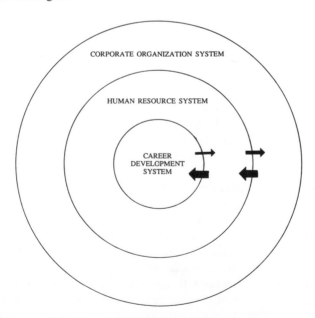

FIG. 2.1. Relationships among systems.

Setting the Stage

The basis of the entire chapter is that an organization is a system in which each element affects the behavior of the whole and is interdependent with every other element (Ackoff, 1981). Thus, the career development system with its objectives and functions operates within the human resource system that, in turn, functions within the corporate organization system as shown in Fig. 2.1. Because a system has a purpose/goal and interacts in its environment, an effective career development system must perform a service that meets a specified requirement of the human resource and organization systems. With this amount of coordination among the systems implied, planning must be interactive and continuous with the various system strategies providing long-term direction.

CORPORATE AND HUMAN RESOURCE STRATEGIC PLANNING

Corporate Strategic Planning

Before identifying the linkage between corporate strategy and career development strategy, *corporate strategy* needs to be defined in terms of its purpose, the process used to develop it, the product of the process, and the implementation required to achieve the intended results. Because a comprehensive approach to corporate strategic planning is not the primary topic of the chapter, we concentrate on those aspects that are, or should be, related significantly to the organization's career development program.[1]

Simplistically, strategic planning produces a corporate strategy that defines a desired state (mission and goals) at some future time and establishes the steps that it will take to get from the current position to the desired one (Tichy, Fombrun, & Devanna, 1982; Walker, 1978). The formulation of strategy not only forecasts a desired end status for each level of strategy and strategic element but also plans the resources that are needed to achieve the goals (end states; University of San Diego, 1984). Strategic planning is an iterative process because, if the essential resources will not be available under any acceptable alternative, the strategic goal(s) need to be modified until they become attainable. A long-range strategy (5–10 years in the future) provides general direction and emphasizes mission and goals. An operational strategy

---

[1] If the readers would like to read texts on corporate strategy and how they link corporate strategy to career development programs, they are in for a rude awakening. Such texts (e.g., Aaker, 1988; Marrus, 1984) spend little, if any, time on human resource considerations in corporate strategic planning and none on developing the workforce required to make a long-range plan achievable.

(3–5 years ahead) is more detailed and focuses on the means to achieve goals by setting intermediate objectives and implementing actions. In addition to goals, the scope of operations (businesses to be in, products or services to be offered, and customer or regions to be served), major competitive thrust (e.g., pricing, marketing, distribution, or service), growth techniques (acquisition, leveraged-buy-out, internal cash flow, etc.), and patterns of resource allocation are identified (Dyer, 1983). For example, new products or technology require research and development that must be planned well in advance of any contribution to a portfolio. The budget cycle of 6 months to 1 year defines specific resource allocation and actions that will be taken. For a small firm or a division of a larger one, a strategy is formulated for competing in a single business element or product and its market. Larger firms cannot stop with a single level of strategy for each business but will need to add a more macrolevel that aggregates and coordinates businesses within a family of them, projecting which businesses to be in (i.e., diversification, product lines, and services). The largest organizations need to aggregate at a third level by coordinating multiple business families via portfolio strategy (i.e., which of its business families will grow, stabilize, or decline at what rates; Eichinger, 1988). Each functional department (e.g., manufacturing and personnel) of a larger, complex organization will develop a strategy that is consistent with the business portfolio strategy.

Most, but not all, strategies contain human resource issues. The turbulent 1980s with their increasing business failures, trade deficits, unfriendly acquisitions, shifts from manufacturing to service industries, and downsizing in traditionally stable employers demonstrate this (Ulrich, 1987). However, corporations may no longer be managed/owned by statesmen that consider employee and national concerns but by those individuals that concentrate on the financial and international arena (Reich, 1988). Without incentives to ensure that American corporations train employees in new skills and increase their adaptability (ability to learn on the job) as well as discover new technologies with broad potential for America, corporations may not adopt such strategies. With this caveat we assume that most corporations are interested in the continuation of the organization and its national base by remaining competitive in spite of the dearth of such incentives.

Competitive advantages, such as low cost outputs, high quality goods, or unique products or services valued by customers, can be acheived via four strategies. The three traditional ones are (a) reducing the break-even cost of producing a product or providing a service that translates into *financial strength*; (b) developing a unique *strategic marketing* capability via diverse products/ services, customer relationships, or market responsiveness; or (c) acquiring *technological or operational capacity* by the ability to build new products/ services more efficiently. The fourth strategy is to build an *organizational capability* that integrates the other three by adapting to transformations in

financial, strategic, and technological emphases. To develop an organizational capability requires the organization first to include within its strategic
planning a definition of its corporate culture, norms, and values, that is
consistent with its strategic goals. Then, the operationalization of that culture
must be planned via formal policies, programs, and practices so that it impacts
on the attitudes and behaviors of the employees across the entire organization (Ulrich, 1987). For example, a "cash cow" business requires the skills and
personal characteristics of a highly efficient, cost-conscious, low-risk, pro-
duction-focused, short-term oriented, stable organization to make it successful.
A preferred supplier/quality business needs personnel that are customer-
oriented, quality conscious, intermediate-term focused, process effectiveness
attentive, and low-risk takers. In contrast, an entrepreneurial business
requires human resources that are oriented toward research, development,
and innovation requiring a long-term perspective, creativity, and risk taking
and can cope with uncertainty because of its need to adapt rapidly to a
constantly shifting external environment to be successful (Govindarajan,
1988; Lorange & Murphy, 1984)

Factors in the external environment that impact on the development of
human resources have significant influence on the organization's corporate/
business strategy and its acheivement (Burack & Mathys, 1987; Fombrun,
1984). *Technological* trends such as the impact of automation in the form of
robotics and computer-aided design/manufacturing affect the rate of introduction of new products, processes, and services, increase the demand for
skilled workers, and, by altering the substance of decision making, reduce the
need for middle management. *Economic* trends such as the international-
ization of markets have caused the United States to move from concentrating
on manufacturing to providing services and raw materials. Thus, high-skill,
blue-collar manufacturing jobs are lost and the number of semi-professional/
white-collar and low-skill jobs increases. *Sociocultural* trends such as the
increasing level of education within a majority of the workforce while the
incidence of illiteracy increases in a significant residual, the changing values
and attitudes of society, the growing presence of women in all facets of work,
and the ageing of a reduced workforce alter the size and composition of the
supply of labor available to the organization. *Political* trends such as the
regulation of environmental impact and employment access, protectionism,
and cooperation among multinational corporations cause job losses in some
labor segments and growth in others. Although the external environment is
important, the internal one also is.

Major organizational strategic factors that influence human resource
career development activities are the corporate culture, structural redesign,
technology, patents, production capability, sales methods, distribution methods, natural resources, products/services, market requirements, size/growth
considerations, and return-on-investment/profit goals (Burack & Mathys,

1987; Tregoe & Zimmerman, 1984). Most strategic plans only consider the organization's human resource as a cost factored into projections of return/ profit or cash flow. The hourly payroll is forecasted and a proportion added to account for the exempt and nonexempt salaried payroll. Such a process does not provide adequate information for a career development strategy to be developed. For example, dramatic expansion at Wendy's and K-Mart caused restructuring as did the thinning of middle management ranks at Ford, Sears, General Electric, Chevron, General Motors, Black & Decker, and Owens-Illinois. Moving into totally new businesses such as US Steel into oil, Exxon into computers, and Sears into finance produced a demand for completely new capabilities within their respective workforces. It takes money and time to replace or change the mix of human resource skills and attitudes when the organization, products/services, processes, work, or culture are changing or to add capability when the organization is growing. Productivity drops on a per capita basis when people are learning in contrast to when they are experienced. Thus, additional training, supervision, and operational personnel resources are required to produce the same results that could be provided by an experienced workforce/organization (American Telephone & Telegraph, 1972). If such costs cannot be supported by projected revenues as State Farm found in one instance in which it was planning to expand, the strategic option has to be modified or dropped (Vincent, 1967). With this multitude of factors to be considered, how should strategic planning evolve?

As in any other type of planning, there are four phases in strategic planning (King, 1986). The first step is developing a strategy followed by the second, planning the implementation of the strategy. The third step is implementing the plan, and the final one is assessing the effectiveness of the strategy and its implementation. The majority of organizations, especially smaller businesses, are not involved in any of the four steps. Their do-nothing policies result in crisis management producing lay-offs and early retirement incentives that create long-term human resource problems such as shortages of high-quality personnel (London, 1985). Where at least Steps 1 and 2 are done, human resource planning is typically reactive, aimed at removing deficiencies or serving as a constraint on strategic choices as described by most authors such as Burack and Mathys (1987), Dyer (1984), Eichinger (1988), Govindarajan (1988), Harvey (1983), Ivancevich and Glueck (1986), Kellogg (1972), Stumpf (1988), and Tregoe and Zimmerman (1984). Human resource subsystems often operate in isolation from each other in reactive functions. The establishment of loyal, long-term employee relationships is emphasized along with specialized technical competence or experience rather than supervisory and interpersonal skills. Employees are controlled or monitored with decisions made at a higher level (London, 1985). Starting in the 1960s and 1970s, many progressive organizations have become involved in preactive human resource planning in which change is assumed but without any reference to the business strategy. In preactive planning, the process—rather than the results— of career development becomes the focus with personnel being trained generically and rotated across functions to broaden and make them adaptable. Such a program is built without a foundation based on the organization's purpose and mission and the program disappears during economic downturns. The most appropriate approach is interactive or proactive planning in which the human resource and career development system representatives interact constantly with other colleagues in corporate strategic planning. Human resources then become positive inputs during the strategic planning process recognizing the relationships among elements of the entire system and maintaining the flexibility required in a dynamic situation (London, 1985; Von Glinow, Driver, Brousseau, & Prince, 1983). This process goes a step beyond that described at Honeywell (Boyle & Yelsey, 1986) and State Farm (Vincent, 1967) in which the human resource planners are encouraged not to accept the business plan as a given but to look for mismatches and try to resolve them. Constant interaction is essential because 75%–80% of the strategic decisions are made ad hoc in response to crises or as a result of a special study. For example, activities such as plant closings and divestiture are seldom stipulated in a formal plan (Dyer, 1984).

This chapter provides a limited perspective of the generic process described briefly in the previous paragraphs by focusing only on the contribution of *human* resources in the formulation of corporate strategy and their contribution to the implementation of strategy. Although strategic planning assumes or explicitly operationalizes the culture, norms, and values of the organization, we concentrate on the development of the human resource required to meet the strategic objectives. Because it is an essential link between corporate strategy and career development, human resource planning is introduced, but other human resource factors, such as labor relations, are not covered.

Human Resource Strategic Planning

The most effective way to incorporate human resource factors within corporate strategic planning is to have a member of the human resource planning group and a human resource executive participate as active members of the corporate strategic planning function. The human resource planning group member should chair a human resource task force that represents human resource functions such as career development, compensation, and labor relations to help him or her contribute effectively in the corporate strategic planning process on both formal and informal bases. The human resource strategic planning function contributes to corporate strategic planning in three ways. The first is a proactive way in which data about the organization's projected human resource strengths are provided as an aid in the formulation

TABLE 2.1.
Some Human Resource Planning Elements
of Concern to Career Development
(Current and Projected Status)

National, International, and Regional

Legal: Labor laws; equal employment opportunity/affirmative action; mandatory retirement; Federal Employment and Training Act; etc.

Economics: Labor market costs (salaries, wages, and benefits) for geographic segments.

Competition: Recruitment, employment, and career development policies and practices.

Technology Trends: Magnitude and rate of changes in technology such as computerization and robotics that require new and cause the obsolescence of present technical and professional skills in relevant sectors; investment in research and development.

Societal: Lifestyle and attitude toward work; dual-career families; workforce aspirations/expectations; individual rights emphasis; accommodation of the disadvantaged; continuous development; etc.

Labor Force Demographics: Occupational (technical, professional, managerial, etc.) shortages and surpluses; geographic mobility by labor group segments; changing mix of age, education level, illiteracy, sex, minority groups, etc.; immigration and English as a second language trends; upward mobility of protected classes; etc.

Corporate

Human Resource Policy: Development opportunities; promotion; training; education; mobility; etc.

Organization: Culture; philosophy (centralized/decentralized, integrated/holding company, etc.); age; growth stage; size; technologies; complexity; businesses; locations; etc.

Workforce Characteristics by Key Education/Skill Groups (management, technical fields, professions, etc.): Inventories, including succession plans; age/length of service/retirement; attrition; cost; performance and adaptability; attitudes and perceptions; race/sex/minorities; etc.

Note: Adapted from Boyle and Yelsey (1986) and Gutteridge (1983).

of strategic direction. The second is an interactive one in which forecasted human resource costs and availability are prepared as part of the assessment of specific strategic alternatives. Such data should be provided within the context formed by external constraints such as legal, societal, competitive, and labor force facts and trends in both domestic and foreign environments (see Table 2.1 for a more complete list). The third is to react to the corporate strategic plan and contribute to its implementation (Burack & Mathys, 1987).

An example of a human resource strength that can be used to develop strategic direction is a critical mass of scientific, technical, marketing, or management talent that can initiate new products, manufacturing processes, markets, or expansion. Another example is a reputation in a specific labor market segment as a good employer that allows the organization to acquire the skilled labor force that is needed. A third example is an effective training function that can introduce new members to the unique organization values and operational knowledge that are required. Such human resource planning information and activities provide the conduit for career development to be linked to corporate/business strategic planning.

CAREER DEVELOPMENT STRATEGY

By limiting the chapter to career development, the focus is on specific programs. *Career* itself is a term that implies a long-range, future orientation. Most of us combine the definitions provided in chapter 1 and consider a career as a set or sequence of work roles that are associated with each other in some rational way by common basic skill, ability, attitude, and environmental requirements that have meaning for each of us and span some period

TABLE 2.2
Career Management and Planning Components of Career
Development

Career Development Functions/Activities	
Career Management[a] (Organizational)	*Career Planning*[b] (Individual)
• Employment	• Counseling
• Orientation	—Human resource staff (89%)
—Initial assignment	—Supervisory (56%)
• Assessment	—Outplacement (37%)
—Performance	—External referrals (29%)
—Selection	—Specialized staff (21%)
—Developmental	• Workshops/Training
• Work Experience/Assignments	—Interpersonal (49%)
—Horizontal mobility	—Job performance/developmental
—Career paths	Planning (42%)
—Special projects	—Retirement preparation (34%)
—Coaching/mentoring	—Supervisory counseling (25%)
• Training	—Life and career planning (11%)
• Education	• Developmental Assessment
• Succession Planning	—Psychological testing (35%)
—Skills inventory	—Testing and feedback(33%)
• Reward Administration	—Self-analysis (16%)
—Promotion/demotion	—Assessment center (15%)
• Professional Activities	• Organization Career Information
• Disengagement	(not surveyed)

[a]Adapted from Morrison and Vosburgh (1987).
[b]Frequency of occurrence in 225 AMA member companies taken from Walker and Gutteridge (1979).

of time. When the organization's perspective of a career is taken, there is a hierarchy of increasingly complex requirements (Morrison & Hoch, 1986). Some individuals' outlooks may include sequences of roles that do not have consistent threads of requirements among them (Hall, 1976; Super, 1957) implying no personal strategy or planning. Such seemingly random careers are difficult to incorporate into a discussion of career development because they are interpreted differently by each individual.

Career development can be separated into career management, a set of programs that represent the organization's requirements, and career planning, a set of activities concentrating on the individual member's concerns (see Table 2.2 for a list of the contrasting sets). With corporate strategy representing the macroview of the total future organization, career management becomes the principal representation of career development in strategic planning. Career planning represents a process that can be used to implement career development strategy and is reflected in the strategy by the corporate career development policy/philosophy /statement of values that operationalizes the corporate culture.

Career Development Strategic Elements

The overriding element of the career development strategy is the statement of the organization's corporate career development philosophy—or generic policy. This statement represents the organization's culture that permeates all of its corporate, human resource, and career development strategic decisions concerning what will be done, when it will be done, and how the decisions will be carried out. Such a statement of policy defines whether individual involvement in career development activities such as transfers and special assignments are voluntary or involuntary, career planning is participative or directed, responsibility for career development is the organization's, the manager's, the employee's, or shared, individuals will be viewed as corporate or departmental resources, the primary source of skilled personnel is internal or external, and so on. An example would be the establishment of the entire corporation as an internal labor market that would be searched for potential applicants for every job opening above the entry level. Such a corporate statement of policy then provides a framework for statements of policy at the business (mission) and departmental level. As the level of policy narrows, the statement of policy becomes less strategic and generic and more operational and specific.

The next key component of the career development strategy is the description of the organization's current inventory of human resource capability by critical education/skill, performance, and protected groups. Although such an inventory traditionally considers managerial succession plans, age, and sponsored group representation, it has become especially useful to include major technical/scientific/professional skill groups and staff (support) management as the demands for new products and processes continue to increase. This inventory heavily depends on the adequacy of the organization's assessment and succession planning programs for accurate information. This inventory should be compared to a human resource projection of the status of that resource at least 5 years into the future. The long-range forecast will consider external factors such as legislation and labor supply and assume that the present organization policies, practices, direction, growth, and investment in human resources remain unchanged. Such a projection must include the level at which new personnel are employed, the potential of present personnel, normal turnover, retirements, and internal mobility for each critical group. A contrast of the projected human resource inventory with the human resource requirements imposed by the forecasted impact of the present corporate strategy will bring out potential shortages in human resources that may jeopardize the acheivement of a present corporate strategic element or possible surpluses that can be built on. For example, a surplus of high potential managers makes a growth strategy not only feasible for the business but also helpful in retaining such personnel (Dyer, 1983). Thus, in a proactive way, an effective career development system may make it feasible to adjust corporate strategy to take advantage of human resource strengths where markets can be exploited.

However, it is much more common for the contrast of the projected human resource inventory with the requirements forecasted using the present or a proposed corporate strategy to demonstrate a shortfall in or inappropriate mix of human resource skills. When shortages resulting from a growth strategy are identified, the cost of employing, orienting, and training the additional personnel, and the reduced productivity of present employees while the new employees are developed should be calculated and used with compensation data as part of the evaluation of proposed alternative strategies.

If the mix of skills is inappropriate, it is possible to assess human resource costs for a strategy alternative using either a "make" or a "buy" career development strategy as reflected in the corporate philosophy of conducting business and policy. A buy strategy would be done as discussed earlier when assessing a growth strategy except the costs of disengagement for employees with the wrong skills would need to be added to the employment program along with the resulting effect of lower morale on retention and possibly productivity. A make strategy would require establishing the costs of assessing and retraining or even re-educating redundant employees to provide them with the knowledge required to work in the new areas of strategy. Transfer costs, where applicable, and the expense of developing skills in the new functions should be added although such expenses for present employees will be lower than for new employees because organizational socialization has already occurred. The costs of a make strategy will be partially off-set by lower turnover and continuing or improving morale as demonstrated at Monsanto in its engineering reeducation program.

Traditional approaches to career development look only at knowledge, skill, and abilities (KSAs), but the career development function can contribute to a corporate strategy by developing a new corporate culture. To shift successfully from a stable, cash cow or monopolistic strategy to a growth or competitive one requires a change in every employee's attitude and behavior. General Electric and AT & T are two corporations that have faced such a major switch in their cultures during the last decade.

Assumptions and Requirements

Both the corporate strategic planning system and the career development system are based on specific assumptions or operational philosophies. The assumptions underlying a career development strategy are less adaptable than those that may enter into the corporate strategy. However, they certainly share at least one basic belief: Both assume that it is possible to project and achieve long-term goals (5 years or more into the future). Thus, the organization manages its resources in a planned way and does not rely on opportunistic or fortuitous exploitation of them. For such a proactive style of management to work, both functions must be perceived by line and executive management as staffed by competent staff personnel and must have the direct involvement of executives and line managers who take responsibility for the results.

Although career development strategy and a typical corporate strategy share another common requirement, a significant level of continuity and stability of the enterprise, mission, products, and processes, this is not always true for corporate strategy. A focus on short-term return-on-investment (e.g., the corporate raider/leveraged-buy-out) or a concentration in a highly cyclical/seasonal business (farming, recreation, and construction) provide little continuity and stability. Both cause so much turmoil and turnover within the organization that career development opportunities from the organizational perspective become very limited involving only the few owners/managers/ administrators that provide any continuity and stability. If the corporate strategy includes closing down or significantly reducing the business without changing it, career development loses much of its purpose for the organization (i.e., providing for the adaptability and growth of its human resources).

Both strategies tend to assume that resources are renewable/adaptable and assets of the organization, but this is not always true within corporate strategic planning. A corporate strategic emphasis on short-term return-on-investment creates the impression that human resources are a cost of operating the organization that should be carefully controlled and minimized. This is a contrast with treating people as an asset that can grow and contribute to the success of the organization via judicious reinvestment as represented in a carefully integrated and designed career development strategy. The organization that is in a business, such as envelope stuffing or mini-mart sales, requiring very low, continuing levels of skill that are acquired readily from the local labor market and are quickly and cheaply trained to reach acceptable performance is not a good candidate for a career development strategy. In such an instance, high personnel turnover produces little extra cost and minimal inefficiencies. There are minimal opportunities for vertical or horizontal mobility and technology does not change rapidly enough to require retraining. Any career development that is needed is individualized for the owner/manager who provides the continuity for such an enterprise. Such an individual can develop within the job as the products/processes/ markets change or the business grows.

Neither corporate strategic planning nor career development strategy should stand alone because they are systemic in nature, relying on the integration of multiple objectives, resources, policies, programs, and functions to be effective. There are corporate strategies that focus almost exclusively on the manipulation of financial resources. Such strategies treat assets such as businesses and human resources as short-term investments making the strategies incompatible with corporate career development strategies.

Although implementing a corporate strategic plan may require resources in the form of discretionary time, money, and opportunity, this varies with the strategic plan. Cost reduction or business closure strategies minimize the requirement for such resources. However, implementing any career development strategy, even job rotation, special project assignments, or reading, incur some cost in resources above those required for the organization to survive making a complex career development strategy impractical.

When a Career Development Strategy is Not Feasible

There are times in which it is not feasible to link career development strategy with a corporate or business strategy (Dyer, 1983). An obvious common one is when corporate management has *no strategic orientation,* choosing to operate in an ad hoc manner and letting strategies emerge out of their day-to-day decisions. In other instances, corporate management *centralizes* its handling of all major strategic issues, including human resource development, and is not willing to share its plans. In each case, the only career development program strategy that can be used is a reactive one in which issues are handled as they arise. In such instances, the appropriate career development strategy is to concentrate on the business and function level in the organization. Those career management programs should be implemented that have a short-term pay-off and can be readily adapted to shifts in the business strategy. Appropriate career management programs that could be emphasized are employment, orientation, developmental reassignments (horizontal mobility), promotion from within, and disengagement. Inappropriate career management programs would be developmental and selection assessment, career paths, and education. Career planning activities are difficult to conduct beyond those that focus outside the organization or develop general personal skills. Examples of the former are outplacement counseling, retirement preparation, life planning, and professional activities. The latter consists of interpersonal skill training.

A third situation occurs when the corporation is configured as a *holding company* and managed wholly in terms of its immediate value in financial resources. In such a case, human resources are only of concern in terms of their cost. The only issue is the maximization of short-term return-on-investment via reducing/controlling costs and the buying and selling of businesses, plants, products, and subsidiaries. Such a strategy is inimicable to career development practices because such long-term investments would not be considered cost effective and in the immediate interests of the stock holders. The only career management programs that could be implemented would be those that make an immediate contribution to the day-to-day business and accrue no costs beyond normal operating expenses. Some examples would be promotion from within and supervisor coaching. If a financial holding company is managed with a longer range perspective, the career development strategies are abdicated to the level of each subordinate function.

DIFFERENT CAREER DEVELOPMENT PRACTICES
FOR DIFFERENT BUSINESS STATEGIES[2]

Because there are situations in which a career development strategy is not practical, the next step in the logic is to propose that career development strategies should vary within different corporate/business strategies. Prior to continuing with the description of these differences some assumptions need to be clarified. A corporation can manage raw materials, products, and financial resources in an integrated manner but leave human resource management decentralized to the function level. An example would be an integrated oil company in which the production, transportation, refining, and marketing functions each have separate human resource policies and programs except for those with direct financial impact such as benefits and pay.

---

[2] For an alternate view of this issue, refer to Stumpf and Hanrahan (1984).

If this is true for your organization, then the following business strategy level issues need to be adapted to the function level. Here it is assumed that all resources within a business are managed with a similar perspective; a perspective that is consistent with an effective career development program as discussed previously.

We are also assuming that a *vertically integrated corporation*, as described in the oil company example, can be treated like a single product/process firm as long as its raw materials, processes, products, and customers are relatively similar in nature. *Diversifying horizontally* into other forms of energy, such as coal, would meet this criterion but into petrochemicals may not because the markets may be too different. If plastics products are produced, the organization becomes a *conglomerate* and should be considered to be in two different businesses. It is proposed that a conglomerate sets the stage for delegating much of career development planning to its subordinate businesses by providing policy and a strategic direction. However, it must service some of its own human resource development needs by developing future members of its organization who are promoted from the businesses. Thus, corporate executives and candidates for such positions become grist for succession planning, assessment, developmental assignment, reward, and education programs.

In essence, we are assuming that different businesses pose different demands on their human resources, especially management, professional, technical, scientific, and skilled blue-collar employees. Such employees are adaptable, if selected and developed to be, given adequate time and a situation in which the change is feasible, acceptable, and not extreme. For example, changing a large plant from producing low- to high-quality products will take several years, not several months; converting a research and development laboratory to a quick response technical service/consulting organization may not be acceptable to a large proportion of its scientists; and expecting mechanical engineers to become astrophysicists would be too extreme a transition.

Practices Common Among Strategies

After the statement of assumptions sets the stage for the discussion of varying career development practices according to the different business strategies, some practices that are common to nearly all strategies are introduced to provide parsimony to the material that follows. As shown in Table 2.3, employment and orientation are two career development processes that are common to all business level strategies except decline. (The latter strategy should restrict the organization to its present employees; see Table 2.3.) The process and standards used in employment and orientation should provide a clear introduction to the organization's philosophy about its human resources and its way of doing business. If mechanistic adherence to detailed policies and regulations are required, as in government, the employment and orientation processes should accurately reflect such an environment. For example, extensive forms, checklists, and form letters plus detailed position specifications, description of benefits, and multiple-choice tests should prevail over interviews, group discussions, team-oriented exercises, and rotational assignments that could be used in an organic system that would be present in some plants and research centers. The emphasis on quality in a unique product strategy, ambiguous sets of tasks and long work days in a growth strategy, and the insecurity of cyclical businesses should be made clear as early as recruiting and continued throughout employment and orientation.

The cost of developing policy and making rewards compatible with strategically consistent developmental behavior is minimal once the organization is oriented in this direction. Unless this is done, a career development program is doomed to failure because it will not produce the desired results. For example, most organizations reward potential as well as performance but the reward for potential should not be made unless specific developmental actions are taken that are consistent with organization requirements and its business strategy. Such actions may include special projects, transfers, and training.

The application of the remaining career development practices should vary in concert with the related business strategy as depicted in Table 2.3. The first strategy discussed is the one in which the business dominates its market with a generic product/service.

Practices Varying by Different Strategies

Dominant Position Generic Product/Service Strategy. When in a dominant (industry leader) position with a generic product/service in a stable market, the organization needs to reinvest its profits, manage its costs and efforts, and innovate effectively to maintain its position. A strong cash cow position provides the funds to upgrade its products/services and assets, including human resources, consistently. Thus, the organization is normally in the position where it can adopt new practices that require a longer than average term to achieve an acceptable return-on-investment. Performance and selection (employment and mobility) assessment can be designed and implemented in a systematic sophisticated manner. The financial assets may be available to conduct developmental assessment programs such as assessment centers. Such programs can be tailored to the organization. Although this description at one time fit a corporation such as IBM best, it can also describe monopolistic organizations such as utilities and even government if the reference to profits is deleted.

Although coaching/mentoring and special projects programs can be provided in most organizations because of their relatively low development and administrative costs, the stability of a dominant position organization makes other systems feasible. Succession planning can be done, making career paths definable and horizontal reassignments effective as developmental processes (Table 2.3). Because the majority of career development results from work experience (Morrison & Brantner, 1990; Morrison & Hoch, 1986), a complete program emphasizing work experience/assignments should be emphasized whenever they are operationally feasible and adequate funds are available. The cost–benefit ratio is high.

When the funds are available, the organization has a clearly defined culture that aids it to accomplish its purpose, and its work is not so simple that the required knowledge and skill can be acquired quickly and accurately at work, training expenditures have an excellent cost-benefit ratio (Table 2.3). Such training needs to be provided as effectively as possible and the results must be applied immediately on the job. However, it is much more difficult to justify an educational program that is not job and organization specific. For senior personnel, it may aid in introducing executives to a relevant network of executives from other organizations providing intelligence from the external environment.

Professional activities are essential to the professional, scientific, and technical employees that must help the organization be technically current and project the direction it should take. Such activities provide the life blood that keeps the organization competitive. Thus, the cost–benefit ratio of such activities for key personnel is high.

Developmental counseling by trained, specialized staff who are aware of not only available career development options but also the business strategy can aid materially in individual career planning (Table 2.3). Skilled counselors can aid individuals to compile operationally feasible and relevant plans leading to successful completion of the activities vice frustration from failing to complete unrealistic goals (Table 2.3). An effective program of developmental assessment makes the career counseling program much more complete and useful (Table 2.3). The provision of timely, relevent organizational career information via a publication like *Perspective*, the Navy's bimonthly career newsletter for officers, helps prepare individuals for planning their careers. Each of these activities can be supplemented by training programs that aid individuals in their career planning and prepare others, such as supervisors, to assist them. The cost of such programs is high but results in terms of operationally effective career plans and the commitment of individuals to their careers in the organization make them worthwhile if funds are available. Each of the career planning practices discussed here is described in order of its priority. However, it is difficult to involve employees in developmental counseling without a complimentary developmental assessment process.

TABLE 2.3

Career Development Practices Appropriate to Different Business Strategies

Business-Level Strategies	Career Development Practices[a]													
	Career Management										Career Planning			
	Employment	Orientation	Assessment	Assignments	Training	Education	Succession Plan	Reward Admin	Professional	Disengagement	Counseling	Training	Dev Assesst	Career info
Stable														
Generic product service	A[b]	A	A	A	A	M	A	A	A		A	M	A	M
Dominant position	A	A	M	M	A	Q	M	A	M		M	Q	Q	M
Minority position	A	A	A	A	A	M	A	A	A		M	M	M	M
Unique product service														
Growth														
Rapidly expanding market	A	A	M	M	A	Q	M	A	M		Q	Q	Q	Q
Stable market	A	A	M	M	M	Q	M	A	Q		Q	Q	Q	Q
Decline														
Divest										M	M		M	
Close down										A	A	M	M	
Cyclical[c]	A	A	A	A	A	Q	M	A	Q		M	M	M	M

[a]Refer to Table 2.2
[b]A = Appropriate. Meets employee and business requirements and costs are acceptable.
M = Marginal. Benefits are acceptable but costs are deciding factor. May partially implement.
Q = Questionable. Benefits are marginal and cost probably too high.
[c]Applies to permanent staff only.

42

Minority Position Generic Product/Service Strategy. The second strategic position, providing generic products/services in a highly competitive market, requires a different emphasis in career development. A minority position in a stable market for a generic product/service indicates that competition is more intense than it is for a dominant or monopolistic organization. The constant effort required to maintain its position requires greater marketing expenditures and attention to keeping costs down than a dominant organization requires. Thus, less funds are available to put into new product and process development as well as human resource development. (Refer to Table 2.3 for the following discussion.)

With the restricted level of available funds, succession planning, assessment, and assignment career management programs become limited in scope. Performance assessment needs to be done but a system tailored to the organization may not be affordable and selection and developmental assessment may be limited to unsophisticated practices such as supervisory judgment. Even though costs must be kept down, supervisory and management training should be conducted to systematize such practices. Otherwise, the contribution of the practices that are implemented will be minimized. Succession planning should be done but should be limited to a few key positions.

Training is required to maintain the competitiveness of the organization but with the available funds limited, careful needs analysis must be done to ensure that the resources are used where they will provide the greatest benefit. Providing organizational support for education may be difficult to justify, but the reward system may be used to encourage employees to participate in educational programs on their own. Promotion, reassignment to key positions, and other decisions could be partially based on educational achievements that are of value to the organization.

A minority position organization probably does not have its own specialized professional, scientific, or technical staff making the support of professional activities irrelevant. Such an organization probably purchases such services on an ad hoc basis.

Limited funds are probably available to aid employees with their career planning. Counseling may be limited to that provided by the human resources staff and supervisors who may receive little, if any, training. Career information may be provided via special sections in media that are already produced by the organization such as periodic newsletters. Career planning or facilitation training and organizationally aided developmental assessment probably can not be justified financially.

Unique Product/Service Strategy. The third strategy, providing a unique product/service, introduces a new dimension to the mix of career development practices that should be offerred. An organization with a unique product/service, such as 3M's "Post-it" brand note pads, aims at a specific market and emphasizes quality at an acceptable cost. This requires major, continuing expenditures in product/service/process innovation and marketing and reduces the funds available for career development. With the organization so dependent on its human resource for implementing its strategy, the need for effective career development practices is as great as it is for an organization in a dominant position in its market. The primary difference is in the content of the practices where constant quality and innovation are emphasized and become enculturated in contrast to cost control. (Refer to Table 2.3 for the following discussion.)

With a quality and innovation strategy, professional activities need major support to create an innovation/quality culture and produce the results that make the products/services unique. Such uniqueness is what differentiates the organization's products/services from potential competition so the risk is high if the activities are not supported.

Although funds that can be invested in career planning practices are probably somewhat limited, they should not be cut off. Quality and innovation are heavily dependent on the contribution of each employee and career planning practices can support such an ethos. Some career counseling may be offered via the human resource staff and supervisors but it should be supported by well-designed training in job performance/developmental planning and supervisory counseling and developmental assessment through simple but quality self-analysis via testing and feedback programs. Timely, relevant organizational career information can be provided via special sections in media that employees receive systematically from the organization. Quality career planning programs will be consistent with the culture that the organization should establish while the simplicity of well-designed programs can keep the costs low.

Rapidly Expanding Market Growth Strategy. When rapid market growth is anticipitated, the key factor in planning career development programs becomes time, because there is little available. (The supplier of air bags for occupant resraint systems in automobiles will be in such a situation as new regulations take effect.) Funds may be present because cash flow can be high when competition is somewhat limited and the market grows rapidly but human resources normally can not be hired and trained fast enough to keep up with the demand for their time. Using a reward system to compensate personnel for constant job rotation and specialized assignments that demand inordinant extra effort not only helps fill gaps but also aids in the development of employees as the need for senior personnel increases. Hiring a majority of the people for senior positions from outside lowers the morale of employees and dilutes the organization culture that initiated the growth in the first place. Short, task-specific training programs can reduce the inefficiencies of a work force that is constantly moving. An assignment to any position probably should be no less than eighteen months considering the benefits required by both the employee and the organization to justify the cost (Morrison & Brantner, 1990). Periodic audits should identify key employees and provide judgmental assessments to ensure that sufficient numbers of capable employees are being prepared to staff the expanding human resource requirements for senior personnel. (Refer to Table 2.3 for the following discussion.)

Time is just not available for attendance at educational programs. The primary exception to this is in professional activities in a high technology business. There the technology of the product or service must be kept state-of-the art or the organization's competitiveness in the market will wane. Focused professional activities are required to keep the professional and scientific staff in a leadership position.

Career planning programs are very questionable because of the ambiguity presented by an organization that is in constant flux and is focused on short-term actions because of its rapid growth. The risk of achieving adequate benefits via career planning are very high.

Stable Market Growth Strategy.   The situation is very different when the organization proposes growing within a relatively stable market. It is deciding basically to wrest a portion of the market away from its competition. The techniques required to do so (i.e., lowering price, establishing product/service differentiation, or increasing quality) are all expensive. This leaves limited financial resources for designing and implementing career development practices (see Table 2.3). The needs for succession planning, assessment, developmental assignments, and training are still present because the organization plans to grow. However, financial resources to apply to human resource development will be limited so nearly the same considerations hold that were presented for a rapidly expanding market growth strategy. The principal exception is training because the number of new employees probably will be relatively small. Very careful needs analyses will need to be done to obtain an adequate return on the investments in training. The primary emphasis in such training probably should be cost reduction if prices are to be lowered or quality improvement if quality is to increase. Any investment in education programs is as questionable within this strategy as it is within a minority position strategy in a stable generic product/service market. (Refer to Table 2.3 for the following discussion.)

Unless product/service innovation would be introduced to beat out the competition for a larger share of the market, supporting professional activity is questionable. Even though the costs are low for professional activities, the need within organizations that do not depend on constant up-to-date professional and scientific innovations is even lower.

With such a dearth of available funds, it probably is unrealistic to expect the organization to divert funds into any career planning programs. Cost reduction/control becomes a constant major daily concern for all employees in such an organization. Career planning will need to be initiated by the employee with informal support from supervisory and human resource personnel.

Cyclical Markets and Project Business Strategies.   The approach to career development strategy must shift markedly for organizations that operate within cyclical markets, such as Christmas holiday sales, and ad hoc projects, such as relocation service and construction. In most cases, their work is tightly scheduled and is completed within a short period of time, anywhere from a few months to a few years. The number of employees waxes and wanes as the schedule requires, producing only a few that are permanent and can be considered a long-term resource or asset. Because such key personnel are critical to the success of the organization, career management of this select group is very important. Research cannot be conducted effectively in an unstable environment so scientists would not be present. Technical and professional personnel are so mobile in an erratic situation that their services may need to be considered temporary although there may be long term requirements for a few of them. Such personnel can be compensated in a way that they can afford to manage and plan their own careers (DeLuca, 1988). As a result, the emphasis in career management should be placed on the permanent staff that can acquire and manage the resources needed to achieve the ad hoc project/task goals. (Refer to Table 2.3 for the following discussion.)

With the limited number of permanent managerial staff being so critical to the ability of the organization to respond to short-term ad hoc demands, succession planning should be done. However, it may not be feasible because of the short-term nature of the business where cycles are not readily forecasted. Thus, careful assessment of who should be considered permanent and specialized programs to retain such people should be emphasized. Providing a variety of work assignments to such permanent staff is important to ensure their adaptability to changing environmental and task situations. As new requirements arise with demanding schedules, training should be provided to get the work off to a smooth, rapid start. In most instances, the work schedule is too tight and unpredictable to provide time for managers to participate in educational programs.

Although career planning programs might make a valuable contribution to the effort to retain permanent staff, it will be difficult to design and implement them. It is very difficult to build programs that respond effectively to such an ambiguous, dynamic business strategy. If career planning programs are to be done, they may need to be innovative and emphasize the development of generic, adaptive abilities in a short-term planning framework in contrast to the traditional long-term, career viewpoint. Assessment to aid individuals in determining if they are working in an appropriate environment and counseling to help them adapt to the ambiguity may be the most critical programs to implement.

Decline Strategies. The perspective of growth underlying career development must change dramatically under a decline strategy. The career development responses to the strategies of organizations that are facing either divestiture or closure of a business are similar, but the content of such programs should vary. It is not appropriate to implement career development programs such as succession planning, assessment, developmental assignments, training, education, rewards, and career information that emphasize long-term concerns. Under decline strategies, the short-term view is paramount. Employment and orientation programs are also not practical because the nature of the new situation is tenuous under divestiture and there is no need for new, permanent employees under closure. As noted at the start of chapter 1. "To not invest in career planning and career development of managers is equivalent to planning to go out of business." In the instance of a decline strategy, that is just what is occurring. (Refer to Table 2.3 for the following discussion.)

The most appropriate response during divestiture is a constant flow of accurate, up-to-date information about the situation. If a reduction-in-force is contemplated, key employees should be apprised of their status so that they do not leave. Programs to aid surplus employees in planning new careers or early retirement, possibly develop new skills, and obtain new jobs should be initiated. Counseling to aid in the adjustment to the new situation is important. The remaining set of career planning programs would not be appropriate because the new owners' business strategy that provides direction for the programs needs to be formulated.

Closure requires specialized programs that provide accurate information about the schedule for closing down and assistance in either adapting to early retirement or obtaining a new job. Because one of the reasons for closure may be obsolescence of the product, process, or service, the employees' skills may also be obsolete. If so, developmental assessment may be needed to aid the displaced employees in determining what new careers or updating might be appropriate and which training/education should be obtained in order to enter the new fields or to become current in the present ones. Because the organization will go out of existence soon, a program for training individuals and supervisors to conduct career development planning in the organization would not be appropriate and, of course, organizational career information is not available.

AN EXAMPLE

The previous section has provided guidelines that can be used in the formulation of a career development function in an organization. It has outlined which activities may be appropriate under different business strategies and how those activities might help form and implement each strategy. In this section, the guidance in the previous one is used to assess what is being done in an exemplary organization and what should be done to make its functions even more effective. *Effectiveness* is defined in terms of the coherence between the career development activities and the organization's strategy.

General Electric

Since 1956, the General Electric Company's Management Education and Research Institute has played an important part in the development of employees. Situated near New York City in Croton-on-Hudson, "Crotonville," its nickname to GE employees, has served as a "clearing house" to transform employees into genuine GE members. Every executive has been required to serve almost 20 weeks at Crotonville (Bolt, 1989). Each chief executive officer has had a specific charter to use the Management Institute as leverage for change while concomitantly developing the career paths of fast-track managers.

In the mid-1950s, Ralph Cordiner used the Crotonville programs to foster change. His decentralization of work functions from the classical hierarchical structures meant that career paths had to be altered radically. Equally important was Cordiner's recognition that managers had to think and act differently in a decentralized environment if delegation of authority and control was to work. As decentralization made corporate structure, communication, and work integration across functions and product lines more unwieldly, Cordiner's successor, Frederick Borg, used executive development as an aid to making the reorganization of GE into 40 strategic business units work (Bolt, 1989). Today, under the leadership of Jack Welch, GE has been transformed from a company with a solid, consistent performance record with strong employee loyalty and brand recognition, into a market-driven, entrepreneurial, high-technology, service-dominant international business. He adopted the Management Institute at Crotonville as a place where "human glue" would hold 14 diverse businesses under a set of common values and a shared vision to be Number 1 or 2, in all of the businesses in which GE chose to compete. This vision required drastic changes in the priorities of each business and in career development strategy. To achieve leadership in market share, many GE businesses had to be transformed. Fix, sell, or close became the operating priorities for the 1980s, which meant delayering and develeving of positions and radically different work structures, ergo new career paths and policies in the businesses.

The career development system at GE starts with a socialization program for all new professional hires, ideally within 3–4 months of hiring. They all go to Crotonville to learn the businesses, understand the strategy, and interface in small discussion teams with business leaders about career paths and jobs within their own line of business. Often this program is capstoned with a visit

Piercy   41-20

A request has been placed on the following item by the patron listed on this paging slip. Please pull this item and forward it to the pickup location given below.

Rockhurst University

Greenlease Library
1100 Rockhurst Road
Kansas City, MO 64110

RU Circ Top Floor

CALL NO: HF 5549.5 C35 C66 1991
AUTHOR:
Contemporary career development iss
BARCODE: 00060101026
REC NO: i16676233
PICKUP AT: EDNWB-Webster

Michelle Piercy
1230 Culverhill Drive
Saint Louis, MO 63119
INSTITUTION: Bridges Cluster
LOCATION: Eden-Webster Library
PATRON TYPE: MOBIUS Graduate

by one of the two vice chairmen providing an early exposure to corporate senior management about careers in GE.

Although there are other training programs within each of the 14 businesses as well as some special job initiation programs (e.g., engineering, manufacturing, information technology, finance, human resources, etc.), Crotonville acts as the company clearing house for all first level supervisors. They attend a week-long residential program about how to manage individual contributors.

As corporate policy has changed, the structure of the company has been reorganized, eliminating several layers of management and providing greater delegation and span of control. Carefully woven into the curriculum at Crotonville is the transformed career path and structure. For example, there is a great deal of emphasis on team development, managing high performance work teams, and managing large spans of control (up to 40 direct reports).

The implication is that there is no orthodox career leader to model. The idea of the generic leader was thrown out with the competitive changes of the 1980s. Managing cross-functional teams, temporary task teams, and relatively autonomous work groups far removed from headquarters support has become the norm. This requires recruiting a highly adaptable, poised workforce. Once chosen and initially socialized, an atmosphere of candid appraisal clearly maps performance and development needs. "Smile" sheets or "wink" appraisals occur less frequently. At first, there were raw feelings and some perceptions of betrayal on the part of old, loyal employees who historically had inflated appraisals. Now they are counseled to improve or be swept away in the vestige of delayering, restructuring, and change.

The steps in the entry sequence of career development at GE seem consistent in a chaotic operating environment. The underlying principles within each step are:

1. Recruit the very best talent from colleges for your entry level training programs (Adams, 1988a, 1988b).
2. Socialize all new professional hires early in their careers by bringing them to Crotonville to meet their own business leaders and those of other businesses and the corporate staff. (This initiates a better understanding of the GE businesses and possible career opportunities.)
3. Introduce all new first-level supervisors to changes in business strategy and the skills required to perform in a manner consistent with the strategy.
4. Train management in finance, marketing, sales, and information management functions.
5. Train technical staff to foster greater skill development and application.
6. Groom fast-track or high potential managers to be business leaders.

The management and executive education and training programs are tied closely to the succession planning process. High potentials who attend these programs are nominated by the businesses and go through a corporate screen. Within GE, Crotonville has historically served as an operating arm for the CEO to introduce his concepts and visions about the business strategy. The curriculum content is adapted to promote new ideas of how to manage a workable career path that supports the operating business strategy.

In addition to Crotonville, GE has developed a highly sophisticated assessment and development process for key managers who are candidates for positions as corporate officers, 150 positions out of 285,000 in the company. The steps in this "accomplishment analysis" system are:

1. Screen an extensive database for key jobs, Crotonville classes, performance appraisals, etc.
2. Using human resources staff, conduct intensive accomplishment interviews with customers, his or her boss, and some work colleagues about key performance and influence behaviors.
3. Compile an inventory from 10 peers and 10 to 20 subordinates about this person's effectiveness as a leader.
4. Meet and discuss with the key general manager about strengths and development needs in the context of career path opportunities.
5. Funnel all of the accomplishment inputs into a narrative profile.
6. Set forth specific recommendations for a development plan with the participant and his or her manager who support or sponsor the targeted changes.
7. In 12–18 months, review the key manager's performance to see if possible derailment factors have been improved prior to advancing the person to corporate status.

GE has pioneered into this career development philosophy the increasingly popular concept that there is no longer job security. Rather, there is career security. One brings talent and experience and is given a level playing field to display that talent.

SUMMARY

The GE example provides an opportunity to summarize the key issues in this chapter by pointing out those represented in both. In GE, career development appears to be a major aid to the CEO in the implementation of the corporate strategy. Although it does not seem that the career development function was a party to planning the strategic change that Welch initiated, a reactive linkage was established between the corporate and career development strategies. The next step would be to move toward an interactive linkage in which career development continuously contributes to and is involved in corporate strategic planning in addition to helping implement the strategy.

The example also provides evidence of coordination among the various career development system elements. Crotonville seems to be a significant ingredient since it presents the corporate culture in orientation and training programs for new members of management from both the external (new professional hires) and internal (first-level supervisors) labor markets. Additional programs continue to contribute to individuals' careers until they become candidates for corporate officer positions. However, recent research has demonstrated that experience, not training and education, is the major contributor to career development (Honeywell Corporate Human Resources Development, 1985; McCall, Lombardo, & Morrison, 1988; Morrison & Hoch, 1986). GE might place greater emphasis on systematic assignment planning (Morrison & Holzbach, 1980).

General Electric's goal to become Number 1 or 2 in each of its businesses places it within several of the alternate strategic positions discussed in the chapter. In some businesses, GE is already in a dominant position, in others it may provide unique products, compete within rapidly expanding markets, attempt to grow within stable markets, or operate matrix organizations managing projects. For the business that does not achieve the goal of being Number 1 or 2 in its market, a divestiture strategy may be implemented. Each different business strategy requires different priorities within the mix of programs[3] in that business' career development strategy and system. The emphasis on career management programs, assessment, work experience/ assignments, training, education, succession planning, professional activities, and disengagement, may vary significantly across the businesses. As discussed in this chapter, contrasts in priorities on career planning programs, counseling, workshops/training, developmental assessment, and career information, may be influenced by differences in the strategies across businesses within the corporation.

A wide variability in career development strategies and programs from one corporation to another and even from one business to another within the same corporation should be expected. The programs present in an effective career development system should interact with and reflect that corporate or business strategy.

---

[3]The huge size and profitability of GE may allow it to do some standardization of its career development systems across businesses because resources may be shared.

ACKNOWLEDGMENT

Appreciation is expressed to Professor Tom Gutteridge and Dr. Jerome Adams for their helpful contributions to and comments on this chapter.

REFERENCES

Aaker, D. A. (1988). *Developing business strategies* (2nd ed.). New York: Wiley.

Ackoff, R. L. (1981). *Creating the corporate future.* New York: Wiley.

Adams, J. (1988a). *Career perception and attitudes of GE new hires.* Unpublished report, General Electric Co., Management Education and Research Institute, Croton-on-Hudson, NY.

Adams, J. (1988b). *Decliner study of GE new hires.* Unpublished report, General Electric Co., Management Education and Research Institute, Croton-on-Hudson, NY.

American Telephone & Telegraph. (1972, June). *Force-loss cost analysis.* Unpublished report, AT&T, Human Resources Laboratory, Human Resources Development Department, New York.

Bolt, J. (1989). *Executive development: A strategy for competitiveness.* New York: Harper & Row.

Boyle, F. A., & Yelsey, A. A. (1986). Human resource planning. In J. R. Gardner, R. Rachlin, & H. W. A. Sweeny (Eds.), *Handbook of strategic planning* (pp. 17.1–17.46). New York: Wiley.

Burack, E. H., & Mathys, N. J. (1987). *Human resource planning: a pragmatic approach to manpower staffing and development* (2nd ed.). Lake Forest, IL: Brace-Park Press.

DeLuca, J. R. (1988). Strategic career management in non-growing volatile business environments. *Human Resource Planning, 11*(1), 49–61.

Dyer, L. (1983). Bringing human resources into the strategy formulation process. *Human Resource Management, 22*(3), 257–271.

Dyer, L. (1984). Linking human resource and business strategies. *Human Resource Planning, 7,* 79–84.

Eichinger, R. W. (1988, April 21). *Aligning executive human resource practices with business strategies.* Workshop presented by the Society for Industrial and Organizational Psychology, Atlanta, GA.

Fombrun, C. J. (1984). The external context of human resource management. In C. J. Fombrun, N. M. Tichy, & M. A. Devanna (Eds.), *Strategic human resource management* (pp. 3–18). New York: Wiley.

Govindarajan, V. (1988). A contingency approach to strategy implementation at the business-unit level: integrating administrative mechanisms with strategy. *Academy of Management Journal, 31*(4), 828–853.

Gutteridge, T. G. (1983, March 21). *Organizational succession planning.* Paper presented at the Chart Conference, Colorado Springs, CO.

Hall, D. T. (1976). *Careers in organizations.* Pacific Palisades, CA: Goodyear.

Harvey, L. J. (1983). Effective planning for human resource development. *Personnel Administrator, 28*(10), 45–52, 112.

Honeywell Corporate Human Resource Development. (1985). *The job and relationships study: A summary of the January 1985 roundtable conference.* Unpublished manuscript.

Ivancevich, J. M., & Glueck, W. F. (1986). *Foundations of personnel/human resource management* (3rd ed.). Plano, TX: Business Publications.

Kellogg, M. S. (1972). *Career management.* New York: American Management Association.

King, W. C. (1986). Formulating strategies and contingency plans. In J. R. Gardner, R. Rachlin, & H. W. A. Sweeny (Eds.), *Handbook of strategic planning* (pp. 6.1–6.30). New York: Wiley.

Leibowitz, Z., & Forrer, S. (1990). Implementing CD systems: Seven strategies for success. *Human Resources Concepts, 1*(3), 3.

London, M. (1985). *Developing managers.* San Francisco, CA: Jossey-Bass.

Lorange, P., & Murphy, D. (1984). Bringing human resources into strategic planning: systems design considerations. In C. Fombrun, N. M. Tichy, & M. A. Devanna (Eds.). *Strategic human resource management* (pp. 275–296). New York: Wiley.

Marrus, S. K. (1984). *Building the strategic plan: Find, analyze, and present the right information.* New York: Wiley.

McCall, M. W., Jr., Lombardo, M. M., & Morrison, A. M. (1988). *The lessons of experience.* Lexington, MA: Lexington Books.

Morrison, R. F., & Brantner, T. M. (1990). *An experience-based learning model.* Unpublished manuscript, Navy Personnel Research and Development Center, San Diego, CA.

Morrison, R. F., & Hoch, R. (1986). Career building: Learning from cumulative work experience. In D. T. Hall & Associates, *Career development in organizations* (pp. 236–273). San Francisco, CA: Jossey-Bass.

Morrison, R. F., & Holzbach, R. L. (1980). The career manager role. In C. B. Derr (Ed.), *Work, family, and the career* (pp. 75–93). New York: Praeger.

Morrison, R. F., & Vosburgh, R. (1987). *Career development for engineers and scientists.* New York: Van Nostrand Reinhold.

Reich, R. B. (1988). Corporation and nation. *The Atlantic Monthly, 261*(5), 76–81.

Stumpf, S. A. (1988). Choosing career management practices to support your business strategy. *Human Resource Planning, 11*(1), 33–47.

Stumpf, S. A., & Hanrahan, N. M. (1984). Designing organizational career management practices to fit strategic management objectives. In R. S. Schuler & S. A. Youngblood (Eds.), *Readings in personnel and human resource management* (2nd ed., pp. 326–348). New York: West Publishing.

Super, D. E. (1957). *The psychology of careers.* New York: Harper & Row.

Tichy, N. M., Fombrun, C. J., & Devanna, M. A. (1982). Strategic human resource management. *Sloan Management Review, 23*(2), 47–61.

Tregoe, B., & Zimmerman, J. W. (1984, May). Needed: A strategy for human resource development. *Training and Development Journal,* pp. 78–80.

Ulrich, D. (1987). Organizational capability as a competitive advantage: Human resource professionals as strategic partners. *Human Resource Planning, 10*(4), 169–184.

University of San Diego. (1984, October). *Proceedings of the tri-service career research workshop. Vol. 1. Group reports.* San Diego, CA: Author.

Vincent, N. L. (1967, Spring). A computer model for manpower forecasting. In L. A. Crooks (Ed.), *Managerial manpower planning: Proceedings of the Executive Study Conference* (pp. 37–56). Princeton, NJ: Educational Testing Service.

Von Glinow, M. A., Driver, M. J., Brousseau, K., & Prince, J. B. (1983). The design of a career oriented human resource system. *Academy of Management Review, 8*(1), 23–32.

Walker, J. W. (1978). Linking human resource planning and strategic planning. *Human Resource Planning, 1,* 24–41.

Walker, J. W., & Gutteridge, T. G. (1979). *Career planning practice.* New York: AMACOM.

3

A Strategic Appraisal of Organizational Rewards

David L. Ford, Jr.
The University of Texas at Dallas

Rabi S. Bhagat
Memphis State University

Reward systems are one of the most important mechanisms for establishing the direction in which individuals will develop in their work roles. Indeed, the literature in the field of organizational behavior and human resources management provides many powerful examples of their functional as well as dysfunctional role in organizations. However, an analysis of how reward systems can play a strategic role in developing effective career systems is not found in the literature. We start with the basic assumption that a systematically developed and strategically integrated organizational reward system can play a crucial role in enhancing the quality of career development-related processes. However, for this to occur, we need to understand the primary objectives of reward systems.

OBJECTIVES OF REWARD SYSTEMS

Organizations design reward systems to (a) induce individuals to join the organization, (b) motivate attendance and performance effectiveness, and (c) reinforce the organizational structure by signaling to employees the instrumentalities of various valent outcomes (Lawler, 1977).

The mere existence of a formal performance measurement and reward system, however, by no means is a guarantee that favorable results are likely to occur. On the contrary, sometimes such systems can do more harm than good.

In this chapter we explore a number of issues related to the strategic design and implementation of performance appraisal-based reward systems that contribute to long-term effectiveness in enhancing careers. Specifically, the interrelationships among long-term strategic priorities (see chapter 2), reward system characteristics, performance appraisal and measurement, and organizational culture are examined in terms of their implications for the effective management of careers in organizations. The incentives and disincentives of various organizational rewards are also examined.

All societies design various laws and institutional mechanisms and programs that in their turn create the incentives structure in the labor market. Recruitment and career development systems generally reflect the dominant cultural values of the society in which they operate (Schein, 1984). Identification of these values is an important human resource management function. The career development system that focuses on recruitment, socialization, growth and development, retirement, and replacement of human resources, should be adequately integrated with the organization's performance appraisal and reward distribution system. However, rarely does an organization's performance appraisal and reward processes reflect its strategic views of the future (Stonich, 1984). Moreover, the career development system is also left unexamined and unintegrated with the organization's strategic management process. These three systems must be made to function with some degree of harmony with respect to each other in order to enhance long-term effectiveness in all of these processes.

Key matching processes that bring the organization and employees together include performance appraisal (present performance); personnel assignment (reflected in human resource inventories of skills, talents, potential, and so on.); job analysis and job design; job placement and reassignment; organizational rewards (especially promotions, job changes, and unique assignments); education and training; retention programs including alternative patterns of work, organization-sponsored move assistance, dual-career assistance programs; retirement planning and counseling; replacement counseling programs; and so on. Many of these matching processes are designed to link employees at various stages of their careers to various elements of the human resource planning process. Several of these key processes are discussed in greater detail later in this chapter.

In many organizations, the focus of the appraisal and reward systems is often on short-term objectives (e.g., annual, and even quarterly, profits). Such an orientation discourages unit managers from initiating actions that would be strategically effective in the long term but might adversely affect their unit's short-term performance as well as their own personal compensations and immediate opportunities for advancement (Stonich, 1984). Unless the performance appraisal and development systems are made consistent with the long-term strategic view of the organization, such short-term practices are likely to endure. For example, the military is a retention organization that is not generally interested in helping its officers to assimilate with the corporate world in their later careers. Vast sums of money are spent in recruiting competent individuals as well as in training and developing them.

Thus, of necessity, the military must have a long-term strategic orientation about its mission and overall career growth and development of its personnel (Oaks, 1985). However, sometimes emphasis on immediate results (e.g., successful immediate inspection outcomes, physical training test results, and other short-term criteria) can lead to an unfortunate and ill-conceived mix of rewards and compensation schemes that are truly incongruent with long-term career development objectives. There is no doubt that reward systems are often a significant cost factor. Indeed, the pay and related monetary compensation schemes often represent over 50% of a typical organization's operating cost (Lawler, 1984). Thus, it is crucial to carefully analyze the possible consequences of an inappropriate reward system on career development processes. We believe that costs can be managed and controlled if the decision makers are genuinely interested in aligning the long-term strategic growth-related objectives with the human resource planning and career development systems.

STRATEGIC ALIGNMENT OF REWARD SYSTEMS

In Fig. 3.1, we suggest that the success of a strategic alignment of the organization's reward systems is a function of several sets of factors. Figure 3.1 implies that before any strategic plan can be developed in an organization,

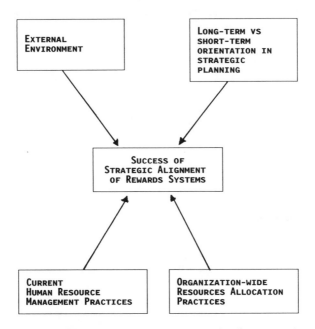

FIG. 3.1. Factors affecting success of strategic alignment of reward systems.

it is important to assess the nature of the present reward system and the kinds of behavior, climate, and structures that have developed in relation to the present reward system. For example, a key consideration might be the nature of the decision-maker allocation rules for rewards (i.e., equity, parity, fairness issues), because these have been shown to influence certain reward outcomes, especially when the nature of the interdependencies among work group or team members varies (Meindl, 1989). In order for these outcomes to be changed successfully, one needs to undertake a strategic alignment of the present reward system with the future objectives of the organization, whether they are growth-related or are concerned with downsizing, and so forth. The external environment acts as a significant factor in affecting this alignment. The nature of current human resource management practices and whether there is a short-term versus a long-term perspective in strategic planning are also important considerations along with the resource-allocation practices in the organization.

The design of reward systems has been dichotomized into process versus content (Lawler, 1984). However, all organizational reward systems possess a third dimension, structure, as well as process and content. The *structural dimension* refers to some of the concrete aspects of the reward system such as the salary structures, the performance appraisal forms, who does the appraisal, and so on. The *process dimension* refers to the nature of communication networks and decision mechanisms that are involved in the administration of the rewards. A critical issue is the degree of openness versus secrecy that exists in relation to how the reward system operates and how people are rewarded. In other words, one needs to be aware of the extent to which the various instrumentalities (e.g., performance—outcome expectations) are both explicit and well understood in the organizational culture. In the following section, we discuss the significance of reward system planning for career developing in organizations.

REWARD SYSTEM PLANNING AND CAREER DEVELOPMENT

In his analysis of how career growth should be examined as a process of identity development through various personal choices that an individual makes, Hall (1986) noted the importance of jointly examining individual and organizational life stages. The notion of organizational life cycle (stages) was developed to delineate the importance of how business firms can match their strategies with the life cycle of the organization (i.e., whether the organization is a new, a mature, or a declining one; Kimberly, Miles & Associates, 1980). This notion of organizational life cycle is also useful in examining career development practices in organizations (Hall, 1987). New organizations are likely to harness the energies of young and growing employees, whereas mature, stable organizations tend to have more older, mid-career employees. The maximum career development is likely to occur only when a person's career cycle is in tune with his or her organizational life cycle. However, if there is some degree of challenge or "stretch" in matching of these two cycles, then it can facilitate even further career growth.

The structure of different types of new rewards that exist in different life-cycle stages of an organization is likely to have a profound impact on its career development processes. However, currently there is very little recognition of the complementary nature of these two important organizational processes. Take total compensation as a case in point. It encompasses the various ways an organization rewards employees. These compensation rewards include direct payments such as wages, salaries, and bonuses; fringe benefits such as vacations, pensions, insurance and medical coverage; and indirect nonmonetary ones such as company cars, various club memberships, and status symbols in the case of many private corporations.

Noncompensation rewards may include key assignments, opportunities for attending various training programs, promotion, security, and the like. One can adopt two distinctly different views in examining these rewards. One view is that they should be designed to primarily enhance future performance levels in the organization. The second view is that employees should be compensated fairly for past contributions to the organization. The first view focuses on the *incentives*, whereas the second is concerned with the notion of *equity* (Peterson & Tracy, 1979). Although these two approaches are not entirely contradictory, they do lead to different emphases on different types of rewards and to different criteria for distributing them. They also have implications for distribution of rewards for different life cycles in the organization. For many individuals, compensation in different forms serves as incentives for certain career decisions such as organizational entry, continued involvement in the organizational role, and so on, irrespective of considerations of continued commitment to a given organization. It is indeed true that rewards that serve as incentives for career entry, such as subsidy for an undergraduate or a graduate program of education, serve as good incentives in enhancing one's future performance as well. The roles that such compensation-based rewards play depends on the efficacy of the match that exists between an individual's career stage and the organization's life cycle. Another consideration that managers might easily overlook is the employee's "equity sensitivity" beliefs (Huseman, Hatfield, & Miles, 1987). A recent study by Miles, Hatfield, and Huseman (1989), based on equity theory, demonstrated that benevolents (who prefer that their outcome–input ratios be less than the comparison other) were inclined to work harder for less pay than were equity sensitives (who prefer outcome–input ratios to be equal) or

TABLE 3.1
A Representative Sample of Career Incentives and Disincentives
Important to Different Career Stages

	Career Stage in Which Important			
	Exploratory	*Establishment*	*Maintenance*	*Withdrawal*
Career Incentives				
• Financial Support for Education and Training		X	X	
• Good pay/compensation	X	X	X	X
• Opportunities for growth and development	X	X	X	
• Opportunities for promotion and advancement	X	X		
• Challenging work assignments	X	X	X	
• Status and prestige		X	X	X
• Good benefits	X	X	X	X
• Chance to exercise leadership/power		X	X	X
• Opportunity to be creative	X	X		
• Visibility/exposure	X	X		
• Autonomy			X	X
• Organizational impact		X	X	X
• Community impact			X	X
• Societal impact			X	X
Career Disincentives				
• Heavy educational requirements	X	X		
• Lack of role models	X	X	X	
• Boring initial assignment	X			
• Heavy demands on time		X	X	X
• Having to compromise personal values	X	X	X	X
• Obsolescence of skills	X	X		
• Required mentorship roles			X	X
• Heavy work commitment			X	X
• Initiation rites	X			
• Inconsistent policies	X	X	X	X
• Limited career options	X	X	X	

entitleds (who prefer that their outcome–input ratios exceed those of the comparison other).

In Table 3.1, we provide a representative sample of career incentives and disincentives that are often considered by managers of organizations and are used in different combinations depending on the life cycle of the organization (i.e., whether it is a new, a mature or a declining one).

The administration of direct type of compensations can take two forms and it depends on the primary orientation of the key managers at a given life cycle of the organization. If the *incentive*-based approach is emphasized then one must decide on appropriate methods of tying rewards to career development as well as future job performance, and devise some effective means for assessing progress in both areas.

On the other hand, if the equity approach is taken, one must identify relevant employee inputs to the job, weight their importance, and find ways to measure them. The plan should also indicate how comparisons are to be made among employees with similar skills and other inputs. It is important to separate compensation and noncompensation rewards especially when making comparisons. Interorganizational comparisons of noncompensation rewards do not appear to be done, but perceptions of fairness in intraorganizational comparisons could play an important role in affecting career development approaches in declining organizations. For example, when some individuals are chosen without any prior justification for certain skill-retraining programs, it does affect the morale of those not chosen who remain unclear as to why and on what basis they were not selected to participate in such programs.

In summary, reward system planning needs to consider the interrelationships among the pattern of organizational career paths; requisite human resource inputs in terms of skills, attitudes, training, and career stages; and organizational life cycles in order to develop the appropriate fit between the reward system and career development system for meeting both short- and long-term organizational objectives.

REWARD SYSTEM'S INFLUENCE ON CAREER MOTIVATION AND PERFORMANCE

Reward systems of organizations represent rich sources of untapped opportunities for developmental sequences needed in the course of one's career. The basic process by which the development of new skills and attitudes occur is best illustrated by the notion of "psychological success cycle" (Hall, 1976, 1986). The essential idea is that an individual works toward a moderately challenging goal and achieves it with some independent effort, receives intrinsic satisfaction and extrinsic rewards (pay, recognition, promotion) and engages in increased levels of effort for enhancing future performance standards. The psychological success cycle explains why it is that success often leads to or breeds future success, especially in career-related performance tasks. We do not go into the details of how this process occurs in this chapter because it is well known in the literature. It is important to note, however, that the notions of feedback and moderately challenging goals are important elements of this process. However, career motivation and subsequent career performance would be adversely affected if appropriate rewards are not available. We believe the following practices can enhance the reward system's positive effects on career motivation, performance and effectiveness.

Career Information Systems

An important feature of this practice is that individuals become aware of more complete and accurate information about career opportunities in their own organizations. As various new jobs are announced in various company publications and individuals nominate themselves for these openings, information about typical career paths into key jobs in the organization is made more salient. Many organizations do not have a well-developed career information system even though it is not costly to put in place. This practice enables individuals to develop their careers in the context of their present organization. It also conveys a clear managerial commitment for the development of internal candidates for job openings that provides higher levels of challenge, feedback, and extrinsic rewards—the elements that can enhance the psychological success cycle.

Career Counseling and Career Pathing

Another important feature that could be incorporated in the strategic design of reward systems is the idea of systematic career counseling and career pathing. Instead of letting job changes be random, unit managers can plan job sequences for employees more carefully. One can move in a logical way when transfers and promotions are being done more systematically with respect to career aspirations of the employees. Some organizations use management development committees to reach managers in their mid-careers and develop 5-year career paths for each middle manager. Individuals with high potential are slated for a series of moves through various departments to prepare them for more advanced level positions. The practice of employing dual-ladder career development in some engineering and research and development organizations is an important improvement in this direction. In these organizations, professionals can advance along either a technical or a managerial career path and receive appropriate training and job assignments that are most relevant to their respective goals. In employing dual-ladder career development strategies, organizations succeed in fostering appropriate levels of career motivation and performance because professionals choose the specific ladder that would indeed enhance their psychological success cycle in the way they see fit.

Opportunities for Skills Assessment and Training

Organizations could use assessment centers to assist development of middle- and late-career managers. When individuals receive opportunities for both assessing and improving their skills, it can become an important form of indirect reward that has the potential to sustain career motivation and performance. Training and career development opportunities for various disadvantaged and minority groups is a good case in point. Affirmative action programs do not necessarily solve the career dilemmas of a vast majority of employees who come from socioeconomically disadvantaged groups. The patterns of historical discrimination that these disadvantaged groups have suffered from in the labor market make many of them deficient in the art of learning new skills that are essential for future career growth and success. When some extra effort is put in designing training programs to enhance their skills, on an ongoing basis, such programs are perceived as being more important rewards than simply complying with affirmative action programs. And as we have suggested earlier, the mechanism with which they operate is the psychological success cycle.

Cross-Functional Movements and Establishment of Incumbency Periods

Although many organizations have traditionally developed individuals through one department or operating unit, there is a new trend toward greater cross-functional movement. Japanese companies practice this job-rotation technique extensively (Ouchi, 1981), and it results in the development of a wider range of skills, a broader network of relationships, and a more companywide perspective. Cross-functional movement is not a straight-forward process unless it is well integrated with the reward system. The movement tends to produce generalists rather than specialists. When specialists are more in demand, such as in technical or research and development functional units, this practice can have some adverse effects. Once again, such practices could be developed if the organization develops a mixed model of specialist–generalist-based career movement paths and tailors its reward system to appropriately match this development. In the mixed model, people might spend a specific period of time (e.g., 5 years) developing as specialists within a particular functional unit. After that incumbency period, they are rotated through different functions and become generalists. This approach of establishing minimum and maximum incumbency periods for specialist and generalist roles satisfies persons' needs for broadening their perspective and prepares them well for general management positions. At the same time, the organization's need for specialists is also met (Hall, 1986).

Breaking Career Routines

Whether it is a cross-functional move or a within-function upward move, there is little substitute for learning that one gets in a new job assignment. In many organizations, because the strategic plans are not integrated with human resource planning, there are often no policies governing how long a person should remain in a particular work role. One notices a greater tendency for mobility in early exploratory years and then it levels off in mid-career, resulting in a career plateau. Such career plateaus produce career routines that comprise a syndrome of habitual behaviors that are displayed in the work role with little emphasis on exploratory or learning behaviors (Hall, 1986). Career routines are established by the cycle of psychological success because it is a self-reinforcing cycle, as success leads to further career involvement and even greater future success. In mid-career, this success cycle can become disrupted mostly due to fewer promotional goals that one has to work toward or because competent performance in one's work role reduces the challenge that one might experience over time. There is a need to break these career routines in the mid-career and establish a new set of cycles of psychological successes (Hall, 1986). Assignment to a new job that would require the learning of new skills and where the network of work relationships would provide a qualitatively different kind of feedback can often accomplish this task of breaking the career routine. Consider the case of a mid-career manager in a high tech company in Dallas who commented:

> it was only when I was transferred to our Saudi Arabian operational unit to manage its operation that I felt a new surge for learning on my job which I had not experienced in my earlier work role in Dallas. I experienced a new set of challenges in learning to function in a new cultural environment and felt that my career advancement was back on track again. (Hall, 1986, p. 129)

In this case, the transfer to an overseas location helped break the manager's career routine. Various incentives in the organizational culture can aid in such new learning that can regenerate a new type of psychological success cycle in mid-career when, as we have argued, past challenges are no longer motivating. The breaking of career routines can also be accomplished through certain assignments that enhance task significance substantially. For example, for a junior officer fighter pilot in the military, assignment as a pilot instructor in "Top Gun," where combat skills are honed, is better than assignment as an instructor in basic flight training. Yet, the latter assignment is preferable to assignment as an officer recruiter. Likewise, for a senior naval officer, assignment as a commanding officer (CO) of a new and sophisticated Spruance-class destroyer is more desirable than assignment as the CO of an older Knox-class frigate. Not only does the officer associate the assignment as CO of a Spruance-class destroyer with a high probability of later promotion, but he also faces a more complex job yielding immediate rewards of high job challenge and status. Assignment other than as a CO at this stage of an officer's career would be a very poor assignment for an officer desiring upward mobility. Thus, the type of assignment not only requires the officer to develop a new set of skills but also has major reward properties (i.e., assignments can be career enhancing and are earned via top notch performance and the assessment of good potential future performance in more significant jobs.) As such, these assignments can play a key role in breaking the syndrome of career routines that may have developed over the years.

CULTURAL INFLUENCES
OF CAREER DEVELOPMENT SYSTEMS

In addition to the strategic design of reward systems to facilitate the process of a psychological success cycle, another type of career environment that shapes a person's sense of career identity and influences career opportunities is concerned with the occupational community and culture (Van Maanen & Barley, 1984). Occupational cultures are work-specific collectives that serve as substitutes for certain benefits that are traditionally found in well-defined community and family structures. These collectives form around the shared identities based on mastery of specific occupational skills and tasks. If one is socialized rather extensively in an occupational community, then he or she is less likely to see one's occupational identity in one specific organization and more likely as part of a broader occupational or professional culture that cuts across many organizations. For example, research and development scientists and physicians derive their identities from the distinct professional culture to which they belong to a much greater extent than they derive them from the culture of their employing organization. What is interesting to note in this regard is that many professionals today are already beginning to identify their career aspirations in terms of the occupational model as opposed to the organizational one.

This approach can result in employees defining the careers more in "protean" terms (Hall, 1976, 1986) and the employees become more like "free agents" in pursuing their career objectives as defined in occupational terms. It is not clear how an organizational reward system responds to such strong influences of one's occupational culture. It may also result in organizational conflicts. Those who view their career as progressing primarily in organizational terms find it difficult to understand the specific types of rewards that are motivating to other professionals who view their careers in broader occupational terms. For example, the scientist that values attending professional meetings and publishing scientific papers may be thwarted in obtaining such rewards by organizational management that perceives such activity as nonproductive or even counterproductive. Such misunderstandings can result in various types of conflicts that can affect career development systems for both groups because scientists lose out on their opportunity to update their technical knowledge and skill, become obsolete, and lower the organization's ability to compete with new technology. Once again, a genuine understanding of the many facets of different occupational cultures in terms of the specific values and attitudinal orientations that they espouse is needed in today's evolving organizations that employ such professionals. Similarly, organizational culture affects one's degree of personal investment in one's occupational role (Maher & Braskamp, 1986).

The socializing influences of organizational and occupational cultures can either act together or against each other and can greatly influence the overall level of investment or commitment individuals will finally bring into their careers in a specific organizational context. If the organization is primarily interested in reinforcing the status quo that exists in the present organizational culture, then it can depend on those employees who view their careers more in *organizational* as opposed to *occupational* terms. Take the military as an example. The military is perhaps a striking example of an organization that uses the reward system very effectively to differentiate between people in different positions and thus reinforce the status quo. Careers are viewed in strictly organizational terms. Each rank in the military has different privileges such as separate officer and NCO clubs and separate housing areas on bases. Such a differentiation, it is believed, serves to make the military more effective because it clearly establishes who has authority and, therefore, it is easier for subordinates to take orders because they come from the position rather than from the person (legitimate power vs. charismatic or expert power). Thus, the whole use of rewards in military organizations is designed to be congruent with the reliance on steep, strict hierarchies with centralized decision making at the top and a single chain of command.

In contrast, the reward systems of organizations where individuals view their careers more in occupational terms are designed to facilitate the fraternal process that is held in high esteem. For example, medical, accounting, or other professions requiring a high level of education and/or licensing exams could be viewed as examples of occupations whose members have more of a "cosmopolitan" rather than "local" orientation to their careers. One recognizes an obligation that goes beyond the simple exchange of one's labor for financial incentives or pay. The strict notion of exchange of contributions for inducements (March & Simon, 1958) does not work well in these contexts. In fact, an organization might need to make its reward systems more amenable for sustaining long-term career growth of the individual even if that means some sacrifice of some short-term objectives.

Opportunities for advancement are often motivated by individuals' needs for development in relation to their careers as opposed to the organizations' needs to fill empty positions or specific slots. In other words, many of the practices inherent in the administration of the reward system reflect a strong commitment for enhancing occupational careers. The idea is that if the organization can succeed in enhancing one's occupational careers, one is likely to contribute more than what is strictly codified in the employment contract.

As we noted earlier, as many contemporary organizations develop distinct needs to employ professionals with specific occupation-based skills, the urgency to tailor their reward system in terms of its suitability for the various occupational cultures involved also increases over time.

INFLUENCES OF SOCIETAL CULTURE

Occupational structure of any society evolves to fulfill the functions needed in the society. This process of evolution is influenced by the cultural values of the society that makes an impact on both the internal career (e.g., the individual occupant's view of his or her own career movement) and external career defined in terms of a socially defined set of steps and requirements for fulfilling a given occupation as well as the amount of occupational prestige that is attached to it. Schein (1984) suggested that cultural variations should be studied with respect to both internal and external career processes as well as with respect to their interactions. To illustrate the distinction, let us consider the actual career steps that are involved in becoming a research scientist in a company. The various steps involved in getting one's doctorate in a given scientific discipline, obtaining postdoctoral training, having patents under one's name, differ to some extent across various societies depending on cultural differences among them. Such differences are likely to influence various steps that are found in one's internal career-related motivation and competencies in terms of how an individual feels about being a research scientist in a company. Career-related motivation, whether it is primarily calculative, altruistic, technical, or economic in nature is judged in terms of the standards of that occupation in a society. These standards are influenced by cultural values of the society, and they, in turn, determine the extent of one's degree of personal joy or dislike in pursuing a given career path.

For some careers and in some organizations, the extent of one's career movement along the three well-known dimensions (e.g., the hierarchical dimension involving upward movement, the functional dimension including the development of specialized expertise, and the inclusionary dimension of assuming greater informal influence and centrality in the organization) is often determined by a number of factors unrelated to one's prior career performance and success. Many professionals who end up being head of some of the important public sector agencies have generally not followed the technical specialist path. Their inclusion in the central decision making units of their organizations, as well as their career progressions, may be predicated on criteria such as age, bureaucratic mentality, family connections, and so on, and have little to do with their professional contributions in a strict technical sense. In some countries around the world, there is an implicit notion that individuals' careers are "owned" by the countries rather than by their individual occupants. This notion is, of course, quite alien to an American way of thinking about careers, but nevertheless it is an important way of organizing careers in some developing countries in the world.

Furthermore, the separation of self, work, and family roles in relation to one's career progression does not follow the traditional pattern one finds in the United States. In the United States, the segregation of these roles becomes more distinct as one's career progresses. One leaves "one's work at the office" more so at the establishment than at the earlier exploratory career stages. However, in some of Asian cultures, there is more of a unity in integrating these roles across one's career span. The part that the reward system plays in facilitating the integration of life roles with career roles is not well understood in the career literature at this point in its development. We believe this area needs considerable conceptual as well as empirical work. Several important areas of inquiry concerning the manner in which organizational reward systems can play a strategic role in shaping career effectiveness are the following.

1. How do expatriates manage their internal careers in a foreign country that might dramatically differ from the United States in the way it defines career success both in internal as well as in external terms? In other words, what can multinational organizations do to facilitate the development of expatriates' careers that will be in consonance with the values of the culture in which they are required to function? The implications for the design of reward systems are not necessarily very clear. The rewards that facilitate culture learning and assimilation in the overseas setting could in fact hinder effectiveness in the back-home setting.

2. What is the significance of various intrinsic as well as extrinsic rewards over one's entire career in different cultures? As we noted earlier, there are no empirical studies of the dynamics of these processes and therefore we can only raise important issues that one should consider in designing reward systems for organizations that employ individuals of different cultural backgrounds. The strength of one type of reward in one culture could be perceived

as being weak in another culture in terms of its innate effectiveness to sustain career motivation and growth.

3. How are career anchors (Schein, 1978) defined and sustained in different cultures? Because the criteria for career success differ across cultures, the notion of what an anchor is and when one might develop a permanent career identity around it will differ across cultures as well. In the United States multinationals, career success is defined more in terms of achievement-oriented, individualistic criteria where as in France criteria concerned with adaptability to organizational change are deemed to be more appropriate (Laurent, 1981).

In terms of Laurent's findings the criteria for career success in the following five western countries appear to be as follows:

United States: Accomplishment of company goals and financial success.

France: Adaptability to organizational change while retaining one's self-confidence and creative mental abilities.

Germany: Creative abilities, one's chronological age, company policies regarding career development.

United Kingdom: Superior's subjective judgment of one's advancement potential.

The Netherlands: One's educational background.

Even though these results are tentative, they suggest the need to re-examine the role of organizational rewards in terms of how career success is interpreted in different countries. Thus, for organizations employing persons from different cultural backgrounds, strong organizational socialization processes may be needed to overcome prior cultural socialization in order for the individuals to have a chance at internalizing the organization's views of rewards in relation to its career development processes.

In summary, we agree with Hall (1986) in restating that the influences at the cultural level have stronger potential for career outcomes than those at the level of the individual—organization interfaces. However, empirical work is almost nonexistent in this area. Unless we have some systematic comparisons of how culture influences careers both in internal as well as in external terms, we are not in a position to make a systematic assessment of the role of organization reward systems in impacting career development systems.

CONCLUSIONS

Neither organizational effectiveness nor individual career satisfaction can be achieved unless there is a better matching of what the organization needs and what the individuals who spend their working lives in those organizations need (Schein, 1978). That is, any human resource planning and development system must be simultaneously concerned about organizational effectiveness, both short and long term, and individual effectiveness and career satisfaction, both short and long term. The reward system that implements the career development system must be consistent with these concerns. With respect to career satisfaction, we previously identified a number of factors in the organizational environment that serve as career incentives and disincentives. It appears that people's perceptions of the career incentives and environmental factors impact not only their decision making process in the *selection* of a career or occupation but also the *future planning* of the career with respect to deciding to sustain growth in that career or to leave it. One's experience in the work organization crystallizes the nature of specific incentives and disincentives in promoting career development. Such experiences also formulate an individual's development of a career anchor early in one's career, which, in turn, might also have important implications for later career development processes. Although the career anchor presumably remains stable over time, it is possible that it might change as well, due to changes in personal interests, needs, and cultural frames of references that exist in one's society as we discussed earlier (Mortimer & Lorence, 1979). It may also change in response to a well-designed reward system that links rewards with the strategic growth of the organization and helps the career incumbents to formulate a focused career anchor when one might not have existed or had existed in a diffuse or vague manner initially. Today's work organizations that are interested in the work commitment, involvement, satisfaction, and performance of its workforce should offer the right mix of career incentives in order to achieve positive outcomes. Individuals are concerned with their own performance, involvement, commitment, and satisfaction and will behave in a fashion that is congruent with the organizational incentives and their own career-related motivations and objectives.

The essential idea behind developing a strategic reward system is to recognize the powerful role of the rewards in sustaining one's occupational and career commitment. Future managers need to also be concerned with the cultural variations in these processes as they design reward systems for culturally heterogeneous groups.

REFERENCES

Hall, D. T. (1976). *Careers in organizations.* Santa Monica, CA: Goodyear.

Hall, D. T. (1986). Breaking career routines: midcareer choice and identity development. In D. T. Hall, Associates (Eds.), *Career development in organizations* (pp. 120–159). San Francisco, CA: Jossey-Bass.

Hall, D. T. (1987). Careers and socialization. *Journal of Management, 13*(2), 301–321.

Huseman, R. C., Hatfield, J. D., & Miles, E. W. (1987). A new perspective on equity theory: The equity sensitivity construct. *Academy of Management Review, 12,* 222–234.

Kimberly, J. R., Miles, R., & Associates (1980). *The organizational life cycle.* San Francisco, CA: Jossey-Bass.

Laurent, A. (1981). *Internal study on career success and concepts of management and organization.* Unpublished manuscript, INSEAD., Fountainebleau, France.

Lawler, E. E., III. (1977). Reward systems. In J. R. Hackman & J. L. Suttle (Eds.), *Improving life at work* (pp. 163–226). Santa Monica, CA: Goodyear.

Lawler, E. E., III. (1984). The strategic design of reward systems. In R. S. Schuler & S. A. Youngblood (Eds.), *Readings in personnel and human resource management* (2nd ed., pp. 253–269). New York: West.

Maher, M. L., & Braskamp, L. A. (1986). *The motivation factor: A theory of personal investment* Lexington, MA: Lexington Books.

March, J. A., & Simon, W. (1958). *Organizations.* New York: Wiley.

Meindl, J. R. (1989). Managing to be fair: An exploration of values, motives, and leadership. *Administrative Science Quarterly, 34,* 252–276.

Miles, E. W., Hatfield, J. D., & Huseman, R. C. (1989). The equity sensitivity construct: Potential implications for worker performance. *Journal of Management, 15*(4), 581–588.

Mortimer, J. T., & Lorence, J. (1979). Work experience and occupational value socialization: a longitudinal study. *American Journal of Sociology, 84*(6), 1361–1385.

Oaks, D. (1985). The transition of women from military services to positions as corporate executives. *Proceedings of the Corporate Linkage Roundtable* (pp. 42–54). Amherst, MA: School of Education, University of Massachusetts.

Ouchi, W. A. (1981). *Theory Z.* Reading, MA: Addison-Wesley.

Peterson, R. B., & Tracy, L. (1979). *Systematic management of human resources.* Reading, MA: Addison-Wesley.

Schein, E. H. (1978). *Career dynamics: Matching individual and organizational needs.* Reading, MA: Addison-Wesley.

Schein, E. H. (1984). Culture as an environment context for careers. *Journal of Occupational Behavior, 5,* 71–81.

Stonich, P. J. (1984, Winter). The performance measurement and reward system. Critical to strategic management. *Organizational Dynamics,* pp. 45–57.

Van Maanen, J., & Barley, S. R. (1984). Occupational communities: culture and control in organizations. In B. M. Staw & L. L. Cummings (Eds.) *Research in organizational behavior* (pp. 287–365). Greenwich, CT: JAI Press.

4

Career Patterns: Mobility, Specialization, and Related Career Issues

H. Dudley Dewhirst
The University of Tennessee

During the 1980s new challenges emerged for human resource managers whose decisions effect organizational policy on career management. Many organizations experienced slower growth, and a significant number became smaller. Thus, upward mobility opportunities declined. At the same time, increasing complexity of managerial and high-technology careers demanded greater levels of expertise and specialized knowledge (Prietula & Simon, 1989). What the 1990s hold in the way of challenges for the successful management of careers cannot be predicted with great accuracy. It is reasonable to believe that career mobility and specialization issues will continue to present important issues for organizational policy makers as well as significant demands on the human resource research community. Policy changes that impact organizational careers, if based on inadequate understanding of career dynamics, can lead to serious organizational performance dysfunctions (Gaertner, 1988).

This chapter reviews career patterns, or the structure of careers. Its primary emphasis is on the objective reality of careers (i.e., the number, type, and variety of positions held in the course of a career). For this purpose, *careers* are defined as a sequence of work activities that are related by organizational content, occupational content, or other characteristic (Morrison & Holzbach, 1980). The focus is on professional, semiprofessional, or managerial careers of individuals within organizations.

The target audience consists of those who manage and those who conduct research on human resource programs, career and manpower planning systems, and management/professional development programs. Thus, an organizational, as opposed to individual, orientation is developed. The more subjective aspects of career (i.e., the attitudes, values, and feelings that individuals have about careers) are not ignored, but are treated as important constraints that the organization must consider in the design of career systems.

The review is divided into two major portions. The first focuses on the basics of (a) mobility, (b) the degree of specialization/diversity, and (c) the overall career pattern that results when mobility and specialization are considered over a full career. The second portion of the review focuses on several more specific problems that organizations face in facilitating the effectiveness of individuals over the full term of a career. These problems include (a) facilitating the transition from specialist to manager, (b) preventing and avoiding technical and other types of obsolescence, and (c) effective management of plateaued employees.

MOBILITY: HOW OFTEN SHOULD ORGANIZATIONS MOVE PEOPLE TO NEW POSITIONS?

There are theory-based models and a modest amount of survey data on the frequency of transfers to different positions. However, there is little research that directly addresses the question of optimum frequency of transfers to new positions. The survey data by its nature focuses on what is, rather than on what should be. Although the desirability of transferring managers for development purposes is often discussed, "There is a paucity of evaluative research, however, assessing the effectiveness of these moves. Indeed, we cannot even tell how often they occur" (McCaffrey, 1981, p. 82). Both common sense and a modest amount of evidence suggests that there are considerable variations between organizations in their rates of internal mobility. Larger organizations and those that are growing rapidly tend to have higher mobility rates. Further, some organizations, believing more strongly in the benefits of job rotation, simply move people more often. IBM is prototypical of such organizations, and many of its members believe that the letters IBM mean "I've been moved."

Managers change positions every $3^1/_2$ years, but there is considerable variation, with 5% moving 18 months and 5% moving only once in 12 years (Veiga, 1981a). However, mobility decreases with age, as was demonstrated in a later analysis of the same data (Veiga, 1983). Mobility as a function of age is shown in Table 4.1 for three age groups (29–37, 38–55, and 56–64). The data

TABLE 4.1
Career Mobility of Managers (Years Per Position)

Age Bracket	29–37	38–55	55–64
Time in first position, years	2.1	3.1	4.2
Average time per position after first	3.1	4.9	8.0

Source: Veiga (1983).

are separated to indicate the time in the first position and average time per position for all subsequent positions. As can be seen clearly, mobility decreases with age. However, some of the apparent decrease is probably a result of both differences in age and differences in overall mobility rates between the time when the older and younger cohorts began their careers. Note that the older group's time in the first position is twice that of the youngest group. It is obvious that mobility opportunities for the age groups were different.

The differences in mobility rates among different age groups is instructive. It indicates that mobility is a function of eras and industries as well as individuals. Careers in boom times and "go-go" industries are characterized by dramatically higher mobility rates. This illustrates that mobility surveys may produce widely varying results and therefore should be interpreted with caution. More importantly, the effect of organizational/environmental factors indicates how difficult it is for an organization to manage the career paths of its members because of its inability to control environmental variables.

A different way to examine mobility is to determine the average number of years spent in each position in a career path. Managers who are over forty years of age spend about $3\frac{1}{4}$ years in their first position, about $3\frac{1}{2}$ years in the second, and somewhat over 4 years in the third position (Veiga, 1981b). After that, some individuals within the sample appear to plateau, so that average times in subsequent positions become less meaningful. However, those that do maintain their mobility, continue to move at roughly a 4-year per position rate.

Mobility rates among military officers are considerably higher than among civilian managers. Command tours for army officers average 18 months (Savage & Gabriel, 1980). Further, officers must expect 20 or more tours in a 20-year period if they are to ultimately achieve general officer rank. Savage and Gabriel argue that this mobility rate is excessive and problems of military effectiveness result from excessively high mobility rates. The rationale is that officers cannot see the results of their actions in such short tours, much less invest effort in solving long-term problems or instituting programs with long-term payoffs.

The disadvantages of high mobility rates are not limited to military organizations. High mobility rates among managers provide incentives for managers to achieve short term gains at the expense of initiatives that would provide greater benefits over the long term (Hayes & Abernathy, 1980). Similar incentives exist for managers to obtain short-term productivity gains by destroying the organization's human assets (Likert, 1961). Paradoxically, organizations with fast-track promotion schemes for star performers may be rewarding organizational destroyers rather than organizational builders.

A theoretical model that focuses on longevity in a particular position postulates three phases of an individuals' experience in each new position (Katz, 1982). The three phases are socialization, innovation, and stabilization. During the socialization period, people are learning what is expected, building social relationships, finding out what is rewarded, and trying to prove their worth. During this period newcomers are not highly effective. This period may last from as little as 1 month to as much as 1 year depending on the complexity of the task requirements of the job and the degree to which previous experience of the individual is relevant to the task requirements of the current position (Morrison & Hock, 1986).

The highly productive period is the innovation phase, a time when the incumbent has become sufficiently secure to fully respond to the challenges of the position. Thus, security and challenge are productively in balance.

However, with the passage of time, employees shift slowly to the stabilization stage. The shift is from high involvement and responsiveness to increasing rigidity in problem solving, greater isolation, selective perception, and a growing reliance on ones own experience and expertise.

This conceptualization would lead one to predict an inverted U-shaped curve when performance is plotted against time in position. Such a curve is shown in Fig. 4.1.

Communication levels and group performance in research and development (R&D) are functions of the average tenure within an R&D group. Groups with an average tenure in the group of less than 18 months and those with more than 5 years are significantly lower in both internal communication and project performance than middle groups that have an average tenure of more than 18 months but less than 5 years. The middle groups also demonstrate much higher levels of internal and external communication (Katz, 1982). It appears that if individuals in groups are moved too often, much of their energy is absorbed in learning the ropes. Conversely, an overly long time in one group leads to isolation and sterility in thinking. One could infer that ideal time per position spans a rather wide range. Translating the average

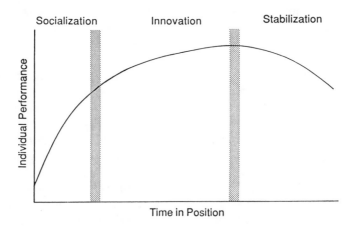

FIG. 4.1. Ideal career structure (from Katz, 1982).

group age into time per position for individuals (this mean, doubling the group age because each group member can be assumed to have completed half of his or her tenure as a group member) suggests the optimum ranges from about 3 years at a minimum to as long as 10 years at a maximum.

When individual performance is measured, rather than group performance, it is highest in groups with an average group age of 4 to 5 years (Pelz & Andrews, 1976). The performance of individuals in younger groups is nearly as high, but falls significantly among groups older than 5 years. The effect of individual age was partialled out, so the results can fairly be attributed to group tenure. The results are remarkably similar regardless of the use of individual or group measures.

The effect of job mobility on performance for professionals other than engineers and scientists is less well known. Comparison of high mobility managers (average time per position of 2.6 years) with low mobility managers (average time per position 6.9 years) reveal no differences in salary or in most aspects of job satisfaction (Veiga, 1981b). High mobiles are more satisfied with advancement, but are less satisfied with their pay. It may well be that high mobility has limited payoffs for most managers except those who ultimately climb to the top of organizations (Veiga, 1981a). This view is supported by Rosenbaum (1979), whose tournament mobility theory suggests that those who reach the top of organizational hierarchies must move early and often. However, more recent research (Forbes, 1987) clearly indicates that the tournament model (i.e., you must win the first round) is less than complete. Positions held later in a career were more predictive of success than were early promotions. Although high mobility may be dysfunctional, low mobility appears to be even more of a hazard. Reducing upward mobility opportunities by hiring outsiders rather than promoting from within can result in significant performance declines (Gaertner, 1988).

Mobility in the form of job rotation is a management development tool used by many organizations. Firms classified as "best managed" by Dun's Review were universally found to believe that most management development occurs on the job, through progressively more responsible job assignments (Digman, 1978). This select group of firms rotates their managers, on the average, every 6 or 7 years.

Mobility in mid- and late-career is clearly related to performance. Among those who ultimately plateau, the poor performers move less frequently at mid-career (Veiga, 1981b). Further, compared with high performing nonplateaus, the poor performers move less frequently throughout their careers after the first two position changes. Unfortunately for organizations interested in enhancing performance through career management of their employees, we do not know if mobility enhances performance or performance enhances mobility. Probably both are true.

In summary, both theory and empirical results indicate that optimum mobility for scientists and engineers is probably between 5 and 7 years, but may be as short as 3 years and as long as 10. It is very clear that transfers every year or two are too frequent for these professionals to learn the ropes and to achieve maximum effectiveness.

There is less evidence concerning optimum mobility rates among managers. Clearly, performance is positively related to mobility in mid- and late-career; however, determining cause and effect is not possible given the nature of available evidence.

It may well be that more frequent moves are appropriate for managers because managerial positions in general require less specialized knowledge than the typical science/engineering position. Optimum tenure in such positions may be more a function of the potentially dysfunctional effects of rapid mobility on the organization (Hayes & Abernathy, 1980; Likert, 1961; Savage & Gabriel, 1980) discussed earlier.

It may well be true that the generally fragmented nature of research on mobility patterns results from a lack of conceptual development in this field. Nicholson (1987) has identified a number of both individual and organizational variables that influence the optimum speed of transitions. More radical changes between highly complex jobs would call for slower transitions. Organizational facilitation, support, and provision of slack raise the benefits of more rapid transitions. Individual success in managing previous transitions, self-confidence, and self-selection for new assignments also allow for more frequent productive transitions. Because specialization or diversity of job content has a major impact on mobility rates, we now turn to the question of specialization and diversity.

HOW SPECIALIZED SHOULD CAREERS BE?

By and large, organizations have not developed policies and practices that govern the degree to which career paths are specialized. Rather, career specialization (or diversity) is largely a by-product of a series of ad hoc decisions made by organizations and individuals. This is true in part because some jobs, or some sequences of jobs require more specialized knowledge and skills than others. Perhaps another reason is that so little is known about the long term effects on the organization of specialized versus generalist career paths. Thus, the approach taken here is to draw inferences on the issue from research in several related areas. It is well accepted that jobs or positions be structured to provide incumbents with enriched jobs—that is, the job should provide skill variety, task significance, autonomy, task identity, and feedback from the job (Hackman & Lawler, 1971). There is considerable evidence that job enrichment leads to higher levels of employee involvement and improved performance. However, the benefits of job enrichment decrease with position tenure (Katz, 1982). Can a move to a new and *different* position provide "career enrichment"?

There seems to be a concensus of opinion that transfers to different positions do facilitate higher levels of performance over the full term of a career. The benefits of job rotation are substantial (Cohen & Meyer, 1979), and the technique is widely used in manufacturing (Robertson, cited by McCaffrey, 1981) and "best-managed" firms (Digman, 1978) as the centerpiece of management development. Transfers to different jobs are major opportunities for personal development (Brett, 1984). A large retailer cut the time required to develop store managers with a career system by expanding the number of career paths with which one could gain the necessary experience (McCaffrey, 1981). The rationale is that career growth requires that people meet new challenges that are within their coping responses (Schein, 1977). However, the need for specialized expertise, much of which can come only through years of on-the-job experience and learning, presents a real dilemma for organizational policy-makers. On one hand, management prizes the contributions of experts who are long-term incumbents in their jobs. Yet, pay and promotion policies pressure individuals to seek diversity in job experience and to move up the hierarchy (Prietula & Simon, 1989). At the same time, company reorganizations, takeovers, and dynamic global competition increasingly result in discontinuous job changes. A study of 10,000 managerial role transitions found that the overwhelming majority were radical changes, with shifts of at least two dimensions of status, function, and organization (Nicholson, 1987).

Within engineering and scientific tasks, diversity of function (technical work, administration, and teaching), in technical work (research, development, or technical service tasks), and in number of specialty areas of research are all associated with high levels of performance (Pelz & Andrews, 1976). It would appear that an interest in delving into many topics (breadth) would produce different results than an interest in probing deeply within a narrow topic. Paradoxically, both interest patterns were associated with high levels of performance among scientists and engineers forty and older (Pelz & Andrews, 1976). This suggests that some individuals are highly effective as specialists, whereas others achieve through more diversified and general careers.

Up to now, this review has been concerned with the degree of specialization that results from job rotation, transfers, and promotions within organizations. There is also a large body of research on occupational mobility that is useful in examining the question of specialized versus generalist careers. *Occupational mobility* is defined simply as mobility between different occupations. Thus, an engineer who becomes a psychologist has changed occupations. This is different in several ways from mobility within and between organizations on which our previous discussion has focused. First and foremost, the occupational shifts generally involve a greater shift of task requirements. The engineer becoming a psychologist involves more change than does the typical intraorganizational transfer that might involve a change from engineering design to technical service. A second difference between occupational mobility and organizational mobility is that the decision is largely an individual one rather than an organizational one (or one that the individual and the organization share). Although a review of this literature is beyond the scope of this chapter, selected findings do suggest partial answers to questions of specialization and diversity or particular relevance to organizational management of careers perspective of this chapter.

More people desire diversity in the form of a mid-life career occupational change than the number who actually make such changes (Sarason, 1977). Numerous studies, based on census data, examine the occupational mobility of working adults. It is well established that (a) there is a fairly high rate of occupational change and (b) there is considerable predictability about the type of change based on personal traits and talents of the individuals involved. Work histories of nearly 1,000 adult men were examined to explore occupational mobility starting with the first occupation after the completion of full-time education (Holland, Sorenson, Clark, Nofziger, & Zahava, 1973). Over 87% were not in the same occupation 5 years later. Others have found that occupational mobility declines dramatically with age; however, it does continue throughout careers. Even among men and women in the 61–65 age cohort, 22% had changed occupations in the last 5 years (Gottfredson, 1977).

A second, and most important point resulting from studies of occupational mobility is that the occupational change is not random, but is constrained by individual interests and values. Holland (1973) has developed a classification scheme for occupations that places all occupations in six broad categories: realistic, investigative, artistic, social, enterprising, and conventional. The classification of each occupation is based on the task environment or requirements of different occupations. In the study cited earlier, it was found that although occupational mobility was high (80% changed occupation), most of the change was within rather than between the six categories of occupational types. Specifically, 77% of all individuals were still in the same category as their first occupation. This result is not affected by the individual's age (Gottfredson, 1977).

Individual differences, defined and measured in various ways, impact on career paths of individuals. Organizations can use Holland's (1973) theory of careers (i.e., the logic underlying the classification of occupations into six broad types) as a basis for career assessment and guidance (Kravetz & Derderian, 1980). The concept of career anchors (the needs, motives, and values that the individual is attempting to fulfill through work) is an alternative means of understanding different career paths (Schein, 1977). The five career anchors are managerial competence, technical functional competence, security, creativity, and autonomy/independence. These anchors represent different "master motives" for careers. Central to the career anchor concept is the idea that a major task of individuals is to discover their career anchor and build their career about it. Different anchors result in career paths that differ rather dramatically in both the frequency of moves and whether the career follows a specialized or generalized path.

Cognitive style is another individual difference variable that influences whether individuals pursue careers as specialists or generalists. Individuals who are systematic thinkers tend to pursue specialized career paths in engineering, production, and management science. Intensive thinkers choose open ended, unstructured professions such as journalism, law, arts, and the like (Keen, 1977).

Differences in vocational interests influence whether individuals remain on specialized career paths or shift to more general and diversified careers. Within a technical organization, those promoted into managerial career paths have different interests than those promoted into specialist career paths. Those promoted to a managerial career path have high scores on Strong Vocational Interest Blank (SVIB) subscales for production manager, army officer, and air force officer and relatively low scores on a technical interest composite of SVIB subscales (mathematician, chemist, engineer, physicist, and architect). Conversely, those promoted to a technical specialist career ladder have relatively low managerial interest subscales and relatively high technical interest subscales (Rosen, Billings, & Turney, 1976).

In summary, when generalist versus specialist careers are contrasted, it appears that individuals do seek change and diversity in managing their careers as individuals. However, for most individuals, there are constraints on the amount of diversity sought. Finally, it is clear that individuals vary rather widely on the degree to which they seek diversity as a result of different cognitive styles, values, vocational interests, and motivations.

Organizations would seem to have several options in dealing with the specialization issue. They could "develop multiple ladders and multiple reward systems to deal with different kinds of people" (Schein, 1982, p. 6). Alternatively, organizations could opt to push individuals in the direction of more general careers on the basis that the competent generalist will remain professionally more useful to the organization over time than will the specialist (Shapero, 1985). However, it is argued that our organizations should reward specialists more so as to keep them in specialists positions where they are uniquely valuable to the organization (Prietula & Simon, 1989).

TOWARD OPTIMIZING CAREER PATTERNS

Having examined the factors of mobility and specialization/diversity in careers, we now turn to a more global view of career patterns. There is an obvious problem in matching organizational and individual needs in career patterns. Examination of the factors influencing intraorganizational mobility (Anderson, Milkovich, & Tsui, 1981) indicates that environmental, organizational, and existing workforce characteristics interact with the individual characteristics, perceptions, attitudes, and behavior of employees. The resultant interaction is a set of opportunities and vacancies, criteria for mobility, and the objective reality of mobility, namely; the rate, direction, and pattern of promotion and transfer. Organizational vacancies and individual mobility are always in balance in the sense that demand is ultimately met by individuals to fill the positions. However, most would agree that the ability of organizations to optimize this supply/demand balance is both difficult and, by and large, undeveloped (Burack & Mathys, 1979; Chicci, 1979; Leach, 1980; Lopez, Rockmore, & Kesselman 1980; Miller, 1978; Sarason, 1977; Von Glinow, Driver, Brousseau, & Prince, 1983). Further, career patterns often reflect an organization's ad hoc human resource solutions to business problems (Gaertner, 1988).

It seems appropriate, therefore, to present a model of the ideal career structure that is adapted from Pelz and Andrews (1976). It is based on considerable empirical evidence gathered in a study of some 1,500 engineers and scientists in a variety of organizations. The basic thesis is that successful, productive careers result when there is a creative tension between security and challenge. First an individual needs a sense of security that is brought about by successful performance in one's work, as well as the self-esteem, self-confidence, recognition, and reputation that grow out of increasing competence. To balance that sense of security there is a need for the challenge of new and unfamiliar problems, exposure to other's ideas through extensive communication and technical debate, and a diversity of assignments and areas of specialization. Career growth results from the creative tension between security on one hand and challenge on the other. Too much challenge can overwhelm the individual who is not fortified with security, self-confidence, and successful task experience. Conversely, too much security, without the stimulation of challenging new assignments and tasks, exposure to new problems and people, leads to isolation—an unproductive retreat to routine thinking, yesterday's ideas, and excessive reliance on tried and true methods.

The ideal career model shown in Fig. 4.2 is adapted from Pelz and Andrews. Ideally, a career should be a series of positions that maintain a balance between the security (brought by competence and success) and the challenge and stimulation of new problems, ideas, and people. The circles in Fig. 4.2 represent successive positions in a career; the horizontal lines represent the growth of individuals resulting from success and increasing ability; finally, the vertical segments represent the increased challenge of new positions in a career. The ideal career, in terms of this model, is represented by the solid line that tracks the career path in which individual growth is

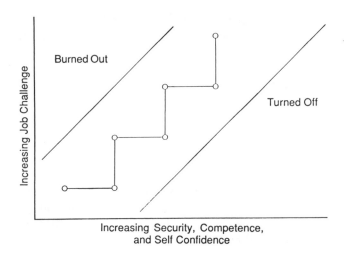

FIG. 4.2. Ideal career structure balances job challenge with personal development (adapted from Pelz & Andrews, 1973).

matched by increasing challenge. The ideal career results as long as the career path remains within the two diagonal lines that mark the boundaries of the area in which security and challenge are balanced. Below that diagonal area, individuals become turned off because their growth and development exceeds that demanded by their job. Conversely, in the area above the diagonal band, the individual is overwhelmed and ultimately burned out by positions with dramatic increases in challenge that are not matched by a sufficient increase in the capability of the individual.

Several important points can now be made concerning the frequency of moves to new positions. The first is that the appropriate frequency of position change depends on (a) the degree to which positions present new challenge, (b) the speed with which individuals grow in competence and self-confidence, and (c) individual differences regarding the felt desirability of specialist versus generalist roles.

One could visualize then a number of different career paths that balance security and challenge. More frequent mobility would be appropriate if either (a) the differences in challenge between successive positions is relatively small, or if (b) the individual grows rapidly in competence and self-confidence. Conversely, slower mobility would be appropriate if positions represent larger increases in new challenge, or if individuals are developing competence more slowly.

Turning from the ideal model to the reality of actual career patterns in organizations, it appears that there is an immense variety of actual career patterns. Further, there is relatively little research on career patterns. One obvious need in this area is a taxonomy of career patterns.

Several different patterns have been identified in the literature that might serve as a starting point for a more comprehensive taxonomy. They are as follows:

traditional vertical,
trunk and branch,
planned rotational,
dual ladder, and
multiple track.

The majority of career patterns fall within the first three, whereas the latter two are special cases that occur in a limited set of organizations. In spite of its relatively limited application, more has been written concerning the dual ladder than any of the other patterns.

Traditional Vertical

The traditional vertical career pattern is one in which one enters the organization in a particular position and whatever mobility occurs is vertical. In small organizations, the traditional pattern results in situations in which the only opportunity for promotions occurs when one's superiors leave their positions through promotion or retirement. The vertical pattern is believed to be the predominant career pattern (Leach, 1980). The traditional career pattern is illustrated in Scholl's (1983) study of career lines in two large Savings and Loan organizations. In one organization some 17 positions were found to lie on five fairly distinct and separate vertical paths up the organizational hierarchy. There was minimal crossing between career lines in that only 7% of the employees were, at the time of the study, on a career line different from the one on which they started. This study points out the classic problem with vertical systems. Upward mobility is limited because (a) some career lines of progression stop at fairly low levels, (b) there are a high number of individuals competing for few promotions as the organizational pyramid narrows, (c) immobile superiors block upward mobility, or (d) outsiders are hired to fill upper level positions. Problems of this type increase turnover (Scholl, 1983) and adversely affect morale and performance (Gaertner, 1988).

In vertical systems, the one line of progression is well known and incumbents will calculate the odds and make their decisions accordingly. Vertical systems work fairly well when organizations are growing because of the increased potential for upward mobility. However, for stable organizations, and especially for declining organizations, the calculus of opportunity is not only vivid, it is often bleak. On the positive side, vertical systems provide individuals with specialized knowledge and facilitate the development of expertise. Further, managers who have progressed vertically are more likely to know their subordinates jobs and understand the technical problems associated with tasks.

Trunk and Branch

The trunk and branch career pattern is, as the name suggests, a more elaborate pattern of career mobility best depicted by the trunk and branches of a tree (Martin & Strauss, 1956). Thus, career patterns in an organization are not simple vertical career lines, but rather only begin as vertical with multiple opportunities for branching into different functions or specialities. Each branch has its own line of progression and possible further branching. The advantages of this system over the strictly vertical model are obvious. Both individuals and organizations have more flexibility. Individuals can influence their career path so as to avoid blockages and/or achieve a better match between their interests and their work. Organizations can shift their human resources more easily, and provide alternative paths for individuals. Although more flexible than the traditional vertical pattern, the trunk and branch pattern can result in problems because mobility is limited to movement along the existing branch patterns. Because some branches do not go far or get clogged, problems somewhat similar to those of the traditional vertical pattern result. A yet more flexible model is needed to depict situations in which mobility potential between branches is possible (Vardi, 1980).

Planned Job Rotation

The two career patterns already described here represent what are, more or less, natural or unplanned systems that result in certain career paths. That is, as vacancies occur, the organization makes an ad hoc selection to fill the position. Without centralized control or influences, the selection will almost invariably be someone in the same vertical line or within the same branch as the vacant position.

In terms of the physical pattern of mobility, planned job rotation is a trunk and branch system with mobility across branches. It is labeled *planned job rotation* to emphasize the requirement for more centralized career planning and control that make mobility between branches a reality.

The purpose of planned job rotation is to broaden the experience of employees and to prevent people from becoming stuck in a vertical career line behind an immobile boss. Managers are told that when new employees are assigned to their organization they will be there for a limited time. I experienced such a system when starting as an engineer in an oil refinery that was part of a large oil company. The company treated engineers as engineers, largely irrespective of whether they were chemical, mechanical, civil, or electrical engineers. After an initial assignment, usually in one's area of academic training, engineers were considered to be refinery engineers, and were systematically rotated between a wide variety of positions. Such cross-functional rotation continued as engineers were promoted into managerial positions. Transfers from managerial positions often included moves into logistics, economic analysis, marketing, and other functions. A major advantage of this system is that one retirement at the top of the organization can result in a number of promotions as well as three times as many lateral moves as the effects ripple through the organization.

Beyond testimonials, which generally proclaim the virtues of such systems, there is little published on such systems. One exception is Digman's (1978) previously cited survey of management development methods used by "best-managed" organizations. That survey found planned job rotation for purposes of developing breadth to be an integral part of the development programs of all the surveyed firms. Even so, empirical research demonstrating the influence of such systems is lacking.

Such systems provide breadth of experience, and tend to prevent individuals from getting stuck or becoming lost or forgotten in a position. However, mobility can be overdone with the result that individuals may never get substantive feedback regarding their work if moved too often. Also, subordinates may rightfully complain about bosses who do not understand their job or who do not provide adequate technical leadership (Blau, 1989).

Dual Ladder

Dual-ladder systems provide that employees, after one or more initial assignments, select or be selected for one of two very different career paths. One path is managerial, whereas the second is a specialized technical or professional path (Hallenberg, 1970). The rationale for this system is that organizations need both managers and specialists. Corresponding to this dual need are competent individuals with different interests and talents. Some want to pursue careers as technical specialists, others want to use their specialist skills as an entry into a managerial career. The dual-ladder system provides a separate line of progression for the specialist that has both the status and financial rewards comparable to the managerial career path. At its best, the dual ladder provides the organization with both managers and specialists. The dual ladder system is said to prevent the conversion of good specialists into bad managers (Moore & Davies, 1977). Because individuals can earn both promotions and pay in either career path, it follows that individuals will select (or be selected for) the path that best fits their interests and abilities. Most of the research on dual ladders has been anecdotal—describing its introduction and utility in one organization.

Results have been mixed. Dual ladders have been judged successful for scientists at Westinghouse (Hallenberg, 1970), Union Carbide (Smith &

Szabo, 1977) Mobil Oil (Meisel, 1977), and Rohm and Haas (Emmons, 1977). On the other hand, significant difficulties and problems are reported at American Cynamid (Cantrall, Manly, Schroeter, & Wakeham, 1977), Amoco Research (Schroeter, 1977), and in an unnamed organization studied by Ritti (1971). The successes tend to have in common several characteristics that their proponents believe are essential for effective dual-ladder systems. First, the criteria for appointment must be made clear. Most authorities suggest a peer review system to select among candidates for the technical specialist ladder. This prevents the transfer of "flunk out" managers to the scientific ladder. Such practice is a tempting way to find an organizational "home" for poor managers, but it is bitterly resented by scientists because it destroys the value and meaning of the scientific ladder (Cutler, 1988; Meisel, 1977).

A second criterion for successful dual ladders is reasonable balance and equity between ladders. Critics argue that dual ladders serve largely to formalize the inferior status of the specialist (Cleveland, 1989). There should be roughly equivalent salaries and perquisites (Schroeter, 1977). Also, there must be a reasonable number of positions in the specialist track so that the probabilities of being appointed are large enough to be perceived as real. The Union Carbide system has approximately the same number of positions on each career track (Smith & Szabo, 1977).

Dual ladders have been criticized by Ritti (1971) as being inappropriate for most organizations. His argument maintains that organizations cannot separate technical and administrative duties. Thus, the dual ladder serves only to formalize the powerlessness of the technical specialist side of the ladder. Ritti's survey data indicate that, at least in this one unnamed organization, those on the managerial ladder enjoyed greater power, prestige, recognition, salary, advancement potential, and the chance to make important technical decisions. This research was done in an engineering development organization, and suggests that dual ladders may have utility only in organizations that have tasks requiring high levels of special knowledge or skill (e.g., fundamental research) that can be pursued in relative isolation without the need for detailed coordination. There is evidence, however, that indicates that dual ladders do result in an effective division of the organization's most competent people into two groups. One group consists of managers with interests, values, and skills appropriate to that role. The other group has greater interest in technical things, but is less interested in, and less competent at people managing skills (Rosen, Billings, & Turney, 1976).

Multiple Career Path System

The final career structure is one that is observed primarily in the military. This pattern involves career assignments in a primary area (such as infantry unit commander or submarine officer) that are interspersed with assignments in a secondary area (such as public information or personnel). This multiple career path allows the military to maintain an experienced cadre of officers for combat command should the need arise while providing manpower for support functions when the nation is not at war and the size of combat forces are relatively small (Morrison & Cook, 1985).

In the early stages of military careers most assignments are in the primary career area (e.g., combat unit command or staff position). In the later career stages, more assignments are made that place the officer in a second functional area (e.g., personnel). Research on the military's multiple career path indicates that such multiple career paths must be extensively supported with career path opportunity information, educational opportunities and careful selection of individual based on interest of the individual in the subspecialty, or second career field involved (Morrison & Wilcove, 1989). There appears to be no closely analogous civilian career patterns. Retail stores often offer managers a choice between a store operations function and a merchandising function. However, most retail managers, perhaps after some early career trial and exploration, tend to stay in one function or the other. Some professionals such as lawyers, doctors, and accountants shift between the functions of practice, teaching, and administration. However, the specialty underlying all is the professional training, and the shifts are often accomplished by changing organizations, unlike the military two-function career.

In concluding the discussion of career patterns, it is obvious that little research has been done that examines the different career patterns offered by organizations. One of the most immediate research needs is for a taxonomy of career patterns. There are a wide array of career patterns between the traditional vertical pattern and the planned rotation pattern, especially for careers in which there are a large number of moves between positions. If a typical manager occupies between 6 and 12 positions in the course of a career, there is a very large number of possible career patterns. Some careers follow essentially vertical career paths. Others would seem to involve specialization early in the career and diversification later. The opposite pattern, that is, early breadth and later specialization also seems to occur. Also important in such a typology is degree of specialization. It is one thing for an engineer to design a variety of products requiring a wide range of engineering skills. It is quite another for that engineer to become a corporate planner, personnel manager, financial analyst, marketing manager, or research director.

RELATED CAREER ISSUES

The remainder of this chapter explores several career issues that are related to mobility, specialization, and career patterns. The first of these issues is that of transition from the role of specialist or independent professional to the role of manager. Next, problems of obsolescence and plateauing are discussed.

Transition From Specialist to Manager

The transition from specialist role to that of manager often creates problems for the individual (see Minor, Slade, & Myers, chapter 5, this volume) for an in-depth discussion of transition problems from an individual perspective) making the transition as well as the organization. Professionals (e.g., doctors, lawyers) experience this difficulty more than quasiprofessionals such as engineers and accountants (Raelin, 1984a). Further, in occupations classified as nonprofessional (e.g., real estate, insurance), entry into management is generally easier.

Specialists can be classified with respect to the ease of transition to managerial roles. The following classification was developed for scientists and engineers at NASA and the National Institute of Health (Bayton & Chapman, 1972).

Type I: Those with "managers motivation" who welcome a move into management.

Type II: Those with "specialist motivation" who are somewhat reluctant to become managers, but adapt to the role after transition.

Type III: Those with "specialist motivation" and who strongly oppose transition. This individual is likely to be frustrated and dissatisfied in management role.

The existence of Type III individuals strongly suggests that management roles are not for everyone. Although different researchers who have explored this topic use varying methodologies and different terminology, there is widespread agreement on this point. Differences in motivation predict differential success in both professional and managerial roles (Miner, 1977, 1980). Using a projective sentence-completion methodology to measure the "motivation to manage" and "professional motivation," Miner (1977) found that managerial motivation is related to success in managerial roles. Those high in "professional motivation" are more successful as university professors. However, the "motivation to manage" measure does not differentiate between more and less successful professors.

Orientations or interests as well as motivations differentiate between specialists and managers. Engineers with technical orientations tend to perform roles such as idea innovator, independent contributor, and technical support roles, whereas those with people orientations are more often found in managerial roles, involved in sponsoring, coaching, and mentoring of younger professionals (Bailyn, 1982). Professional and managerial values are related to organizational roles of NASA scientists and engineers. Those in managerial roles have higher managerial orientations and lower professional orientations than young nonmanagers with 1–3 years of service. However,

TABLE 4.2
Skills Likely to be a Source of Difficulty in the Transition to Manager

	Percent Having Difficulty
Operating within the system:	
Organizational	44
Financial	30
Personnel	30
Working with diverse people	30
Coordinating group effort	28
Decision making	12
Problem solving	4
Related areas technology	4
Fundamental technology	2

Source: Bayton and Chapman (1973).

among nonmanagers with 4–5 years service, the average professional has higher managerial and lower professional orientations, indicating that the socialization process has changed the orientation of these professionals. Interestingly, the same approach in a smaller organization with less of a managerial culture indicated little, if any, early career change in orientation (Dewhirst, 1970).

It seems that research evidence from a variety of approaches indicates that individual differences of several types indicate that a large proportion of early career specialists do have the motivations, orientations, and interests which facilitate the transition to management and help them to perform well in that role. Approximately 65% of the engineers and scientists at NASA and NIH are capable, by virtue of their interests and motivation, to successfully make the transition to manager (Bayton & Chapman, 1972).

Selection of appropriate individuals to make the transition would seem to be the first step in a program to facilitate effective transition. Assessment centers are a most promising aid in selection of managers (Badawy, 1983). Trial managerial assignments, personality tests, measures of interests, motivation, and interpersonal skills are potential aids to effective selection. Discussion of the wide array of selection methods that exist is beyond the scope of this chapter. Suffice it to say that there are many methods that have been used with reasonable success. Although none are perfect, and virtually all have their critics, it is abundantly clear that careful selection facilitates effective transitions to managerial positions.

The problems that individuals experience in transition are related to three broad areas: (a) understanding and being able to operate in a larger, more complex system; (b) dealing with people; and (c) relinquishing the specialty. Problems with organizational systems (budgetary, financial, and personnel) are the primary source of difficulties in transition for scientists and engineers (Bayton & Chapman, 1973). Other significant problems arise for new managers in coordinating group effort, working with diverse people, and so on. Except for a small minority of managers, problem solving and decision skills as well as knowledge of basic technology and related areas are not a problem. Sources of transition difficulty found by Bayton and Chapman are shown in Table 4.2. Transition problems of an administrative systems nature are also emphasized by Badawy (1983). Low levels of strategic thinking are a significant cause of problems in transition (Krembs, 1979). Thus, there seems to be a reasonable consensus that understanding the system, both in operational and strategic terms, is a major problem.

People problems cause major problems for the new managers. In addition to the findings of Bayton and Chapman (see Table 4.2), "low relationships orientation" (i.e., poor people skills) is a major contributor to transition problems (Krembs, 1979). A large number of skills relating to people management such as leadership, communication, conflict resolution, sensitivity to emotions, motivation, and so on are major contributors to transition problems (Badawy, 1983).

The third area of difficulty in transition is that of giving up the specialty work and the values that are inherent in the specialty. Technical competence is a major source of status and prestige among professionals (Allen, 1969). This strong ego identification with technical competence results in too much involvement in technical details by the manager (Krembs, 1979). The problem is more likely to be a matter of values rather than of competence. That is, the new manager knows what should be done, but simply does not do it because of a preference for specialist tasks over managerial tasks.

Organizations can facilitate the transition to managerial roles in many ways. These are summarized in Table 4.3 and are discussed here. A preview or trial experience as a manager cannot only help individuals decide whether to accept a managerial position, but also provides a learning experience (Krembs, 1979). Orientation programs that focus on how organizational systems work with an emphasis on the clarification of authority, duties, and responsibilities can also aid in solving transition difficulties (Badawy, 1983; Bayton & Chapman, 1972).

Mentoring and coaching of the new manager are significant aids in the transition process. The mentor role is a major career stage of professionals,

TABLE 4.3
Helping Specialists Cope With the Transition to Managerial Roles

1. Preview experience in managerial tasks
2. Orientation programs
3. Mentoring and coaching
4. Facilitating shifts in values and motivation
5. Management training
6. Management development experiences

and one that facilitates the growth and development of both the mentor and the young professional (Dalton, Thompson, & Price, 1982). Mentoring is strongly advocated as an aid to specialists in transition (Badawy, 1983; Bayton & Chapman, 1972).

Specialists should be helped to make the necessary value and motivational shifts essential for successful performance (Krembs, 1979). Both coaching and management training are largely ineffective until the individual wants to learn the skills required in the new role. Such value shifts are facilitated by investiture processes that demonstrate with some flair the importance of the new role (Van Maanen, 1982). Having a party, sharing organizational secrets, or providing a salary increase demonstrate organizational acceptance and facilitate acceptance of new values (Raelin, 1984a). Closely related to facilitating shifts in values and motivation is helping the employee relinquish specialist duties. Thus, a request for a new manager to personally handle a difficult specialist task, and then praising the result, will discourage rather than encourage the shift in values (Krembs, 1979).

Organizations are often inattentive to transition problems. Young accountants must largely make the transition on their own because of the lack of organizational attention to transition in accounting firms (Greiner & Scharff, 1980). Transition is more difficult in accounting firms because of the (a) emphasis on technical rather than managerial expertise, (b) lack of lasting superior–subordinate relationships inherent in the strong project or client orientation, (c) delegation of many traditional senior management functions to lower levels, and (d) reluctance to create a hierarchy. In combination, these characteristics of accounting firms minimize the value of managerial functions and reduce the motivation for the young accountant to learn them. One recommendation is to create positions that combine some managerial duties and independent professional tasks. These "producing managers" in effect wear two hats (Lovsch & Mathis, 1987).

Organizationally specific management training that focuses on learning how to cope with the organizational budgetary, financial, and personnel systems should be conducted (Badawy, 1983; Bayton & Chapman, 1972; Krembs, 1979). A management development program should combine formal training with developmentally designed work experiences that allow for experimentation, trying out new skills, and gaining insight on managerial problems.

The ability of individuals to cope with and adjust to transitions is underestimated by most organizations. Individuals may be uncomfortable with transitions and may experience significant difficulties. However, that adjustment process has enormous potential for individual growth and development (Brett, 1984). Additional benefits to organizations accrue from organizational change and role development (Brett, 1984; Nicholson, 1984).

Organizations have much to gain from a better understanding and improved management of transitions. Indicative of the current state of the art is Brett's observation that the lack of reliable information about both individuals and jobs results in placement errors. The resulting placement errors, in turn, provide for personal role development and change that would have been foregone had the placement system had the information to accurately match people and jobs.

By and large, what is missing from the previous discussion is empirical research on the specific problem of the transition from specialist to manager. The most researched area is that which identifies individual differences (motivations, orientations, values, interests) that facilitate or exacerbate the transition. Beyond that point, there is little more than survey research on problems in transition. For the most part, the remaining findings and prescriptions, although valuable, are not empirically based. Particularly needed is research to evaluate the effectiveness of the various methods advocated to facilitate transition. The work of Brett (1984) and others on how individuals adapt to career transitions is helpful. However, comparative research on the effectiveness of different transition-facilitating methods within organizations is needed. Additionally, studies comparing transition support systems (i.e., clusters of facilitating methods) between organizations would also be useful. Finally, the question of facilitating changes in values and motivations seems worthy of further research. The desire to become a manager is related to the degree that the organizational climate or culture values the managerial role (Dewhirst, 1989). Thus, it may well be that transition difficulties are related to values embedded in the organizational culture. If so, then changes in organizational culture are needed to facilitate transition.

PROBLEMS IN LATER CAREER STAGES: OBSOLESCENCE AND PLATEAUING

Organizations and those who research them have become increasingly concerned about problems of obsolescence and plateauing. Although organizational researchers have treated these two topics in relative isolation from one another, they are clearly interrelated. Concern for obsolescence and consequently research on that subject predates that on plateauing, although interest in both issues has roots in an aging professional, technical, and managerial workforce as well as a slowing of the growth rate in the economy and in many large organizations. The aging workforce became an issue in the 1960s, stimulating concern over obsolescence. The leveling of growth rates and consequent reduction in mobility opportunities for an older professional managerial workforce came somewhat later, beginning in the 1970s. It became a problem of major significance in the 1980s as many firms experienced downsizing and restructuring. Comparison of research in the two areas reveals differences in terminology but considerable overlap and similarity on issues, problems, and remedies. Our discussion begins with technological and managerial obsolescence, then moves to plateauing, and finally compares the programs and methods to prevent, alleviate, and cure.

Technical Obsolescence

Obsolescence became a problem of real concern when organizations began to have significant numbers of older professionals. For nearly two decades after World War II, growth in both the number and proportion of technically trained professionals kept the average age of engineers in the United States below 40 (Dalton & Thompson, 1971). As the economy and a number of industries matured, the average age of professionals increased. So did research on problems of obsolescence especially when performance of engineers and scientists was found to peak between the ages of 40 and 50 (Pelz & Andrews 1976). Other studies found even earlier performance peaks, and suggested that obsolescence was accelerating (Dalton & Thompson, 1971).

The initial emphasis was on technical obsolescence and the issues were how to update technical professionals with new knowledge and skills that had emerged since they completed their formal education. For example, Rothman and Perrucci (1970) surveyed nearly 4,000 engineers to determine the association between career experiences and technical obsolescence in technical areas studied in school and technologies that had emerged since completion of formal education. Working on technically complex tasks, in research and development functions, and in dynamic industries reduces the technical obsolescence of both types. However, assignments involving primarily administrative duties cause greater loss of in-school knowledge, but help engineers with emerging technology. These results suggest something that many organizations overlook when they attempt to "cure" obsolescence by encouraging employees to take refresher courses. The message is that obsolescence has more to do with use of existing skills on the job and the need to learn and use emerging technologies on the job than does formal coursework. Coursework generally does not help performance, and may well be associated with continuing performance decline (Dalton & Thompson, 1971). Further, comparisons across companies indicate that spending more time and money on continuing education provides no advantage in preventing or curing obsolescence. The general conclusion is that, if obsolescence is an appropriate descriptor at all, it is more motivational than technical. A 2-year study of R&D productivity concluded that "Lack of basic ability seems to be a minor factor in the process of technological obsolescence; conversely, lack of stimulation/challenge/motivation appears to be a major factor" (Ranftl, 1977, p. 27).

What is needed if we are to understand the problem is a broader approach that goes beyond technical obsolescence. The following classification scheme (Miller, 1978) is illustrative of this more productive approach:

inadequate knowledge,

inadequate skills,

failure to adjust and grow,

growth and change away from organizational needs,

decline in energy and motivation,

loss of organizational acceptance, and

diminished need for functional specialty.

The first two are the conventional forms of technological obsolescence. "Failure to adjust and grow," and "Decline in energy and motivation" are the root causes underlying the knowledge and skill obsolescence. Obsolescence can also be caused when the individual continues to grow, but in directions not matching organizational needs.

At the beginning, decline in energy and motivation is most often attitudinal in nature. However, eventually real mental and physical decline result. Obsolescence resulting from purely physiological causes is rare (Shapero, 1983).

The last two causes listed demonstrate that obsolescence is often a result of the organization rather than the individual. This view is supported by Shapero (1983) and Thompson and Dalton (1976). The argument is that there is no such thing as obsolete people, but that something does happen to some professionals in their 40s and 50s that causes them to become unproductive. Thus, obsolescence is a result of plateauing (see the discussion of plateauing by Minor, Slade, & Myers, chapter 5, this volume). In this view, obsolescence is more a result of organizational incentive systems and lack of job challenge than it is of individuals. It is organizations not people who are obsolete (Dalton & Thompson, 1971). Incentive systems that reward predominantly managers tend to brand nonmanagers as losers (Dewhirst, 1971; Prietula & Simon, 1989). Cost systems work frequently against career development because older engineers are kept off projects involving new technology by cost conscious project managers (Dalton & Thompson, 1971). This is because of the older engineers' higher salary and consequently higher overhead charges. There is too much emphasis on product planning and projects and not enough on career planning. This emphasis means that professionals often get "trapped" on a long-term project and do not get the exposure to new technology.

In summary, obsolescence research has broadened its scope over time to include a wider array of causal factors. This broadening has generally found organizational factors, most notably those related to incentives, career opportunities, and career paths, at the heart of obsolescence problems. This has brought obsolescence research to a position very similar to that on career plateaus, to which we now turn.

Career Plateauing

Research on career plateauing is different in several ways from that on obsolescence. First, it is a more general phenomenon, occurring in all organizations and among all levels of personnel, not just professionals with specialized training. Second, plateauing is singularly focused on promotion (or more precisely nonpromotion), its determinants, and results. Finally, there is less uniformity and certainty about what do about plateauing that involves questions of values and ethical considerations. Although there is an unequivocal desire to prevent, alleviate, or cure obsolescence, it is not as apparent as what should be done about plateauing. (See Miner, Slade, & Myers, chapter 5, this volume, for a discussion of the different types of plateauing.)

A *career plateau* is defined as a point in a career where the likelihood of additional hierarchical promotion is very low (Ference, Stoner, & Warren, 1977). The plateau is an inevitable consequence of the pyramid shape of organizations in which the number of positions at a given level is inversely proportional to height in the hierarchy. Every career ultimately plateaus. Nonpromotion sneaks up on most people (Roseman, 1977). It, and the plateau that goes with it, is usually a nonevent and often goes unrecognized. This fact makes research on plateauing more difficult, because classification of individuals as plateauees can often be accomplished only well after the fact. One operational definition of *plateaued employees* is that any employee not having been promoted in 10 years is said to be plateaued (Near, 1983). Although logical, this approach makes empirical research more difficult. Of course, not all plateauing is a nonevent. Failure to be promoted or failure to be selected for certain positions is a clear sign in some organizations. In the military, failure to be selected for certain command positions is a sign that plateauing has occurred, and a failure to be promoted on schedule is apparent to everyone.

The organizational downsizings that occurred with high frequencies in the 1980s significantly constrained mobility opportunity (Hall & Louis, 1988). Although there has been some research exploring the short-term impact on organizational members of organizational decline (Cameron, Kim, & Whetten, 1987; Feldman & Leana, 1989), no empirical work could be found that addresses the long-term impact of decline on careers. However, recent work on job insecurity (which presumably would accompany organizational downsizing and decline) indicates that job insecurity is negatively related to commitment, trust in the organization, and job satisfaction. Surprisingly, no relationship was found between job insecurity and job performance (Ashford, Lee, & Bobko, 1989). Interpretation of these results is problematic because the level of analysis was individuals. Comparisons between organizations in decline and others were not made.

Although plateauing itself is usually subtle, its impact over time is not. It creates a very real, unsubtle problem for individuals and organizations alike. Career incentives change as shown by Roseman's (1977) analysis of differences in motivating factors (Table 4.4). Because most of these factors are recognized as central in the motivation of professionals (Herzberg, 1968), the potential for lowered job involvement is great. Job involvement has been shown to be the single best predictor of productivity (Pelz & Andrews, 1976). Furthermore, deviant behavior often results when career expectations of professionals are not fulfilled (Raelin, 1984b). Thus, the primary concern regarding plateauing is the same as that of the obsolescence; namely, that of declining performance. Terms like *deadwood* or *shelf-sitter* are often used to describe plateaued individuals.

On the other hand, organizations are filled with *solid citizens*, plateauees who do most of the organizational work and probably comprise the largest group in most organizations. This group receives little management attention and is rarely the focus of research (Ference et al., 1977). Professionals frequently make adaptive rather than deviant responses when their career expectations are not fulfilled (Raelin, 1984b). Many, perhaps most, plateaued professionals make successful adaptations to plateauing. Career success and life satisfaction appear to be unrelated to one another (Bray & Howard, 1981). Thus, it is clear that plateauing, in and of itself, is not necessarily negative. Some writers argue that we simply have put too much emphasis on climbing the corporate ladder while many managers would prefer to exercise their competence in staff rather than managerial roles (Schein, 1982). It is also clear that in many non-U.S. cultures, promotion to managerial ranks is

TABLE 4.4
Differences in Motivating Factors
(Promotables vs. Plateaus)

Motivators	Promotables	Plateaus
Rewards	Growing	Plateauing
Status	Increasing	Decreasing
Attention	Continuing	Fading
Challenge	Increasing	Fading
Variety	Increasing	Decreasing
Learning opportunity	Increasing	Decreasing
Security	Increasing	Decreasing

Source: Roseman (1977).

less emphasized (Dewhirst, 1989). Plateauees are not different from nonplateauees on self-reported measures of motivation, job satisfaction, or job performance (Near, 1983). Thus, it seems that plateauing is not necessarily a problem for many individuals.

The mixed responses of individuals to plateauing raises some interesting and unanswered questions. Examples are: (a) whether plateauees should be told they are plateaued or be allowed to maintain hope of promotion? (b) whether acceptance of being plateaued or continuing to aspire for promotion results in better performance (Ference et al., 1975). A more fundamental question: Is there anything wrong if employees are less motivated and less involved as long as they meet organizational standards? (Schein, 1982). Because of ethical or value issues inherent in some of these questions, there are no definitive answers. However, the need for research that compares the results of different organizational treatments of plateaus is much needed to allow better informed decisions by organizations.

THE PREVENTION AND TREATMENT
OF OBSOLESCENCE AND INEFFECTIVE PLATEAUS

There is unanimous agreement that prevention is better than attempts to cure or treat obsolescence or ineffective plateaus. A "negative spiral" occurs when an individual gets negative feedback, is stuck in a dull assignment, or does not get the expected promotion (Dalton & Thompson, 1971). If an initial burst of greater effort does not bring favorable results, then lower self confidence, less effort, and less job involvement result. Once this stage is reached, reversal is difficult. The obvious implication is that organizational efforts directed toward prevention will be more effective than those designed to revitalize obsolete/plateaued performers.

If prevention is a better strategy than treatment., then a large body of literature on effective career management, productive climates, and management development is relevant. Hall's (1971, 1976; Hall & Louis, 1988) "psychological success" model is one example. Another example is the "creative tension" model of Pelz and Andrews (1976) that was cited earlier. Rather than review this broader body of literature, we focus more specifically on work that examines the actions that organizations can take to prevent and/ or better manage problems of obsolescence.

These preventive/curative actions can be classified into three broad categories as follows:

Organizational systems
Work assignments and environment
Individual support

TABLE 4.5
Prevention and Treatment of Obsolescence and Ineffective Plateaus

Organizational Systems

Integrated personnel programs
Assign on basis of career development, not cost systems
Dual-ladder systems
Flexible organizational structures and pay systems
Organizational manpower reviews
Job rotation
Training and development

Work Assignments and Environment

Assignments requiring use of new technology
Job enrichment
Job evolvement
Team work assignments, programmed interaction
Changing work group membership
Recognition, rewards for performance

Individual Support

Performance appraisal and performance counseling
Encouraging individual assumption of responsibility for career planning
Encouragement to try new and different assignments, tasks

The recommended actions in each of these categories are shown in Table 4.5 and are discussed here.

Organizational Systems

There is a clear and pressing need for better integration of manpower planning efforts with performance appraisal systems (Ference et al., 1977), promotion and educational support systems (Morrison & Wilcove, 1989). More integration and better use of the information buried in personnel functions and systems are needed (Hall, 1971). Revising accounting treatment of overhead charges that prevent older (and higher paid) individuals from project assignments involving new technology would result in opportunities for older professionals to learn (Thompson & Dalton, 1976). Increased flexibility is needed in organizational pay systems, with more emphasis on paying for performance rather than position. Loose rather than tight organizational structures would facilitate the assumption of entrepreneurial, mentoring, and other roles often reserved for managers. Along a similar line, the proponents of dual ladder systems (reviewed earlier in this chapter) argue that such systems provide both incentives and recognition for the employee who does not become a manager (Hallenberg, 1970; Kimblin & Souder,

1975). In one study, it was found that adding a third ladder to an existing dual-ladder system provided for higher levels of satisfaction and development for plateaued engineers (Hall, 1985).

A major preventive action is job rotation and transfers. Lateral moves are a way to avoid stagnation and disappointment of plateaued managers (McCaffrey, 1981). Job rotation of ineffective plateaus, or even demotions can have a renewal effect in certain circumstances (Ference et al., 1977). Pushing an engineer between the ages of 35 and 40 into a new field provides renewed enthusiasm (Dalton & Thompson, 1971). Organizational manpower reviews of individual careers and some degree of centralized control is needed if job rotation is to be effective (Thompson & Dalton, 1976).

Although training has been shown not to be effective as a stand-alone treatment for obsolescence, it is still recommended by most authorities. The consensus is that training is necessary, but not sufficient. In combination with other organizational programs, training can be an effective aid in maintaining the vitality of plateaued people. Educational support is a helpful adjunct to the career planning activity (Miller, 1978; Morrison & Wilcove, 1989). Creative approaches are needed in training, such as full time coursework to help engineers learn new technologies and sabbaticals for purposes for retraining and renewal (Dalton & Thompson, 1971).

Continuing development is important and justified for nonpromotables (Roseman, 1977). The emphasis should not be on training (being sent to courses of narrow scope to learn skills of uncertain relevance to one's work) but on development (voluntary, individualized, broader experiences with substantial participation aimed at behavioral change and problem solving). Development is seen as more appropriate and more effective for mature nonpromotable employees, but flexible approaches, such as offering employees a 3-year overseas assignment with their families as a renewal vehicle, are needed (Shapero, 1983).

Work Assignments and Environment

The work itself is the best preventive medicine for becoming obsolete or becoming an ineffective plateauee. Work assignments in new technologies, those that require use of knowledge and skills, and dynamic environments prevent obsolescence (Rothman & Perrucci, 1970). Assignments on multiple tasks (Farris, 1973) that require the use of new technology, even if it is inefficient in the short run (Dalton & Thompson, 1971), provide the potential for renewal. Individuals in particular jobs for long periods of time can gain many benefits of job rotation if their job evolves or changes in ways that better match their abilities, skills, and interests (Estler, 1981). Managers directly supervising working-level professionals should create events that involve people in analyzing their work, setting goals, and designing changes for improvement (Miller, 1978). Managers should also create excitement by increasing the variety of task assignments and sharing with employees information about the importance of their work.

The immediate work group environment is important in creating a productive climate. Intervention of managers and the creation of systems that require teamwork, interaction, and collaboration coupled with reasonably demanding and strong time pressures for the completion of assignments helps maintain productivity (Farris, 1973). Managers should make sure that new people join the group periodically (Katz, 1982). The recognition of achievement is vital to maintaining involvement and interest. Publicity needs to feature the professionals who do the work rather than top managers (Thompson & Dalton, 1976). Of course, internal everyday recognition for good performance is essential (Myers, 1964). Good performance should be rewarded with more challenging work, especially in stable organizations where challenge may be the only reward available (Myers, 1964; Shapero, 1985).

Individual Support

Although most of the important elements of a program were enumerated earlier, there remain several relating to individual encouragement and support. Probably the most important of these is that the organization must make certain that employees know that they must take personal responsibility for their own careers (Miller, 1978). Having said that, it is also important that individuals are encouraged and supported in their efforts to maintain vitality. Self-starters may well take care of themselves, but others need encouragement to try new and different things (Shapero, 1983). Getting people involved in career planning facilitates more effective careers (Gould, 1979). Long-run problems can be avoided with accurate appraisals of marginal or poor performance (Ference et al., 1977). Performance appraisals can be used to engage supervisors and subordinates in discussion and joint problem solving on performance and career issues (Maier, 1976).

NEEDED RESEARCH

The most critical research needs on career structure are discussed here.

Mobility. There is a need to gather and analyze information on performance as related to mobility rates. One would not expect to find a single clear optimum mobility rate. However, within particular careers (e.g., accounting, production management, scientific research) it would seem that optimal mobility rates—or appropriate ranges of mobility rates could be identified. The question of mobility and age needs more work. An overview of the mobility research suggests that in general mobility may be too high in the early career years and too low in the later years. More work needs to be done on the effects of declining mobility opportunities that result from organizational maturity and downsizing. More work is also needed to assess the effects of creative organizational responses to decline such as the addition of a new career path as discussed by Hall (1985).

Specialization.   Clearly, the question of specialization versus diversity interacts with mobility rates. More specialization is required to be effective in the case of a research scientist working at the frontier of a narrow field. In such careers, it is probably true that advances in the state-of-the-art are an effective substitute for a new position, because both provide new challenge. Research is needed to examine this issue.

Finding an appropriate degree of specialization in career fields is needed; however, the search is confounded by apparent very wide individual differences. It seems that a great deal of the research on careers is saying, in a broad general way, that more diversity is needed in careers. The research on occupational mobility, career shifts, and job enrichment all suggest this. Paradoxically, many people are very productive and very happy in careers that involve high degrees of specialization. Work is needed to identify those aspects of either the individual or the work content in such careers which make them successful.

Career Patterns.   This is the most barren of all research areas. For the most part, the actual pattern of careers in many professions and organizations is not known. There is a real need for a taxonomy of career patterns. Once this is accomplished, studies that compare the effectiveness of different career patterns within and between organizations and professions are needed.

Transition to Manager   There is relatively little empirical research on the transition to manager. Survey research is needed to identify transition problems and issues in a wider array of professions. In addition, comparative research is needed on organizational programs to facilitate transition. What methods, or set of methods, best facilitates effective transition? Another question raised by the review in this area is: What is the role of values (e.g., managerial vs. professional) in the effectiveness of transition?

Obsolescence/Plateauing.   The evidence of problems with obsolescence and ineffective plateauing suggests the high potential for research in this area.

Much of the evidence suggests that there is perhaps a need for higher mobility rates among older employees to prevent the stagnation that is the major problem. The research to date seems to identify most of the important causes of and preventive methods to treat obsolescence and better manage plateauees. The problem is that the preventive medicine incurs costs that are obvious, but has payoffs that are both uncertain and long term. Credible cost benefit studies are needed to convince organizations of the utility of such prevention programs.

Systems Approach. Above all, there is a need for a systems approach in designing and executing research on career patterns. Conceptual work by Nicholson (1987) on career transitions provides a useful model that interrelates individual, organizational, and society/cultural variables. Nicholson's model is based on a transition cycle that implicitly calls for longitudinal research. Such models are much needed to guide research for several reasons. First, research that considers both organizational and individual variables will produce improved theory and richer empirical results. Second, longitudinal research is required to produce credible results and more useful guidance for practitioners. As has been pointed out here and elsewhere (Nicholson, 1987), most career patterns result from ad hoc organizational decisions over which job incumbents have little control. Somehow, the short term needs of the organization largely preempt any sense of career continuity, logical progression, and human resource development. To contribute to a more productive balance between individual career development and organizational needs, researchers will need to provide credible research that relates career issues to organizational variables of vital concern to executives.

An example of such a research issue is the relationship between strategic competence of the organization and the priority an organization places on managing the careers of key people. It has been argued that the loss of preeminence in global markets by American firms results from the failure of American firms to develop, nurture, and maintain fundamental strategic competence. This competence resides in the skill and expertise of the workforce (Pralahad & Hamel, 1990). Yet, managers of strategic business units are not required to compete for these vital human resources or report on their stewardship efforts to develop and maintain them. In Pralahad and Hamel's words, "How strange that SBU managers should be made to compete for corporate cash, but never for key people" (p. 87). It is easy to dismiss the corporate concern for cash over careers as short sighted. However, the fact is that research on careers has not produced convincing arguments and evidence to support a different policy. To address such issues in a meaningful way will require research of broader scope than has been typical in the past. Much of the research will, of necessity, be both interdisciplinary and longitudinal. Such research will require sustained funding and the dedication of research teams over a period of time, but the need is there and the payoff is enormous.

REFERENCES

Allen, T. J. (1969). Information needs and uses. In C. E. Quadra (Ed.), *Annual Review of Information Science and Technology* (Vol. 4, pp. 1–29). Chicago, IL: Encyclopaedia Britannica.

Anderson, J. C., Milkovich, G. T., & Tsui, A. (1981). A model of intra-organizational mobility. *Academy of Management Review, 6*(4) 529–538.

Ashford, S. J., Lee, C., & Bobko, P. (1989). Content, causes and consequences of job insecurity: A theory-based measure and substantive test. *Academy of Management Journal, 32*(4), 803–829.

Badawy, M. W. (1983). Managing career transitions. *Research Management, 26*(4), 28–31.

Bailyn, L. (1982). Trained as engineers: Issues for the management of technical personnel at midcareer. In R. Katz (Ed.), *Career issues in human resource management,* (pp. 35–49). Englewood Cliffs, NJ: Prentice Hall.

Bayton, J. A., & Chapman, R. L. Professional development: Making managers of scientists and engineers. *The Bureaucrat, 1*(4), 407–424.

Blau, B. (1989). How IBM technical professionals perceive their work environment. *Research Management, 32*(1), 27–30.

Bray, D., & Howard, A. (1981). Career success and life satisfaction of middle aged managers. In R. E. Hill, E. L. Miller & M. A. Lowther (Eds.), *Adult career transitions: Current research perspectives* (pp. 153–178). Division of Research, Graduate School of Business, University of Michigan, Ann Arbor, MI.

Brett, J. M. (1984). Job transitions and personal and role development. In K. M. Rowland & G. Ferris (Eds.), *Research in Personnel and Human Resources Management* (Vol. 2, pp. 155–185). Greenwich, CT: JAI Press.

Burack, E. H., & Mathys, N. (1979). Career ladders, pathing and planning: Some neglected basics. *Human Resource Management, 18*(2), pp. 2–8.

Cameron, K. S., Kim, M. U. & Whetten, D. A. (1987). Organizational effects of decline and turbulence. *Administrative Science Quarterly, 32,* 222–240.

Cantrall, E. W., Manly, D. G., Schroeter, D. G., & Wakeham, H. R. R. (1977). Success and failures. *Research Management, 20*(4), 30.

Chicci, D. L. (1979). Four steps to an organization/human resource plan. *Personnel Journal, 58*(6), 390–394.

Cleveland, J. N. (1989). *Research needs in the management of concurrent dual career development: Military and industrial findings and research approach.* Navy Personnel Research and Development Center, San Diego, CA.

Cohen, S. L., & Meyer, H. H. Toward a more comprehensive career planning program." *Personnel Journal, 58*(9), 611–615.

Cutler, W. G. (1988). Stalled on the dual ladder. *Research Management, 31*(1), 52–53.

Dalton, G. W., & Thompson, P. H. (1971). Accelerating obsolescence of older engineers, *Harvard Business Review, 59*(5), 57–67.

Dalton, G. W., Thompson, P. H., & Price, R. L. (1982). The four stages of professional careers: A new look at performance by professionals. In R. Katz, (Ed.), *Career Issues in Human Resource Management,* (pp. 129–153). Englewood Cliffs, NJ: Prentice-Hall.

Dewhirst, H. D. (1970). The socialization of the young professional: A study of changes in career values of engineers and scientists during the first five years of employment. Unpublished doctoral dissertation, University of Texas, Austin, TX.

Dewhirst, H. D. (1971). Impact of organizational climate on the desire to manage. *Personnel Journal, 50*(3), 196–201.

Dewhirst, H. D. (1989). *Management in Australia: No worries.* Survey of Business, Center for Business and Economic Research, University of Tennessee, Knoxville, TN.

Digman, L. (1978, Autumn). How well-managed organizations develop their executives. *Organizational Dynamics*, pp. 63–80.

Emmons, W. D. (1977). The pioneering research approach. *Research Management, 20*(4), 27–29.

Estler, S. E. (1981). Evolving jobs as a form of career mobility: Some policy implications. *Public Personnel Management Journal, 10*(4), 355–364.

Farris, G. F. (1973). Motivating R&D performance in a stable organization. *Research Management, 16*(5), 22–27.

Feldman, D. C., & Leana, C. R. (1989, Summer). Managing layoffs: Experiences at the challenger disaster site and the Pittsburgh steel mills. *Organizational Dynamics*, pp. 52–64.

Ference, T. P., Stoner, J. A. F., & Warren, E. K. (1977). Managing the career plateau. *Academy of Management Review, 2*(4), 602–612.

Forbes, J. B. (1987). Early intraorganizational mobility: Patterns and influences. *Academy of Management Journal, 30*(1), 110–125.

Gaertner, K. N. (1988). Managers careers and organizational change. *Academy of Management Executive, II*(4), 311–318.

Gottfredson, G. D. (1977). Career stability and redirection in adulthood. *Journal of Applied Psychology, 62*(4), 436–445.

Gould, S. (1979). Characteristics of career planners in upwardly mobile occupations. *Academy of Management Journal, 22*(3), 539–550.

Greiner, L. E., & Scharff, A. (1980). Challenges of cultivating accounting firm executives. *Journal of Accountancy, 150*, 57–58.

Hackman, J. R., & Lawler, E. E. (1971). Employee reaction to job characteristics. *Journal of Applied Psychology, 5*, 259–286.

Hall, D. T. (1971). A theoretical model of career subidentity development in organizational settings. *Organizational Behavior and Human Performance, 6*(1), 56–76.

Hall, D. T. (1976). *Careers in organizations.* Pacific Palisades, CA: Goodyear.

Hall, D. T. (1985). Project work as an anecdote to career plateauing in a declining engineering organization. *Human Resource Management, 24*, pp. 271–292.

Hall, D. T., & Louis, M. R. (1988). When careers plateau. *Research Management, 31*(2), 41–45.

Hallenberg, E. S. (1970). Dual advancement ladder provides unique recognition for the scientist. *Research Management, 13*(3), 221–227.

Hayes, R. H., & Abernathy, W. J. (1980). Managing our way to economic decline. *Harvard Business Review, 58*(4), 67–77.

Herzberg, F. (1968). One more time: How do you motivate employees. *Harvard Business Review, 46*(1), 53–62.

Holland, J. L. (1973). *Making vocational choices* (2nd ed.). Englewood Cliffs, NJ: Prentice-Hall.

Holland, J. L., Sorenson, A. B., Clark, J. B., Nofziger, D. H., & Zahava, D. B. (1973). Applying an occupational classification to a representative sample of worker histories. *Journal of Applied Psychology, 58*(1), 34–41.

Katz, R. (1982). Managing careers: The influence of job and group longevities. In R. Katz (Ed.), *Career issues in human resource management.* Englewood Cliffs, NJ: Prentice-Hall.

Keen, P. G. W. (1977). Cognitive style and career specialization. In J. Van Maanen (Ed.), *Organizational careers: Some new perspectives* (pp. 89–105). London: Wiley.

Kimblin, C. W., & Souder, W. E. (1975). Maintaining staff productivity as half-life decreases. *Research Management, 18*(6), 29–35.

Kravetz, D. J., & Derderian, S. E. (1980). Developing a career guidance program through the job family concept. *Personnel Administrator, 25*(1), 39–42, 76.

Krembs, P. (1979, November). Making managers of technical gurus. Proceedings for the Public Management Research Conference, Brookings Institution, Washington, DC.

Leach, J. J. (1980). Career development: Some questions and tentative answers. *Personnel Administrator, 25*(10), 31–34.

Likert, R. (1961). *New patterns of management.* New York: McGraw-Hill.

Lopez, F. E., Rockmore, B. W., & Kesselman, G. A. (1980). The development of an integrated career planning program at Gulf Power Company. *Personnel Administrator, 25*(10), 21–27.

Lorsch, J. W., & Mathis, P. F. (1987). When professionals have to manage. *Harvard Business Review, 65*(4), 78–83.

Maier, N. R. F. (1976). *The appraisal interview: Three basic approaches.* La Jolla, CA: University Associates.

Martin, N., & Strauss, A. (1956). Patterns of mobility within industrial organizations. *Journal of Business, 1956, 29*(2), 101–110.

McCaffrey, W. T. (1981). Career growth vs. upward mobility. *Personnel Administrator, 26*(5), 81–89.

Meisel, S. L. (1977). The rung's and promotion criteria. *Research Management, 20*(4), 24–26.

Miller, D. B. (1978, February). *Counteracting obsolescence in employees and organizations.* Paper presented at the 49th AMA Human Resources Conference, Chicago, IL.

Miner, J. B. (1977). *Motivation to manage: A ten year update on the "Studies in Management Education" research.* Atlanta, GA: Organizational Measurement Systems Press.

Miner, J. B. (1980). The role of managerial and professional motivation in the career success of management professors. *Academy of Management Journal, 23*(3), 487–508.

Moore, D. C., & Davies, D. S. (1977). The dual ladder—Establishing and operating it. *Research Management, 20*(4), 14–19.

Morrison, R. F., & Cook T. M. (1985). *Military officer career development and decision making: A multiple cohort longitudinal analysis of the first twenty-four years* (MPL-TN-85-4). San Diego, CA: Navy Personnel R&D Center.

Morrison, R. F., & Hock, R. R. (1986). Career building: Learning from cumulative work experience. In D. T. Hall (Ed.), *Career Development in Organizations* (pp. 236–273). San Francisco, CA: Jossey-Bass.

Morrison, R. F., & Holzbach, R. L. (1980). The career manager role. In C. B. Derr (Ed.), *Work, family and career* (pp. 75–93). New York: Praeger.

Morrison, R. F., & Wilcove, G. L. (1989, August). *Roadblocks to warrior subspecialty development.* Paper presented at the annual American Psychological Association convention, New Orleans, LA.

Myers, M. S. (1964). Who are your motivated workers? *Harvard Business Review, 42*(1), 73–88.

Near, J. P. (1983). Work and non-work correlates of the career plateau. In K. H. Chung (Ed.), *Proceedings of the Academy of Management* (pp. 380–383). Dallas, TX.

Nicholson, N. (1984). A theory of work role transitions. *Administrative Science Quarterly, 29*(2), 172–191.

Nicholson, N. (1987). The transition cycle: A conceptual framework for the analysis of change and human resources management. In *Research in personnel and human resources management* (Vol. 5, pp. 167–222). Greenwich, CT: JAI Press.

Pelz, D. C., & Andrews, F. M. (1976). *Scientists and organizations: Productive climates for research and development.* Ann Arbor, MI: Institute for Social Research, University of Michigan.

Pralahad, C. K., & Hamel, G. (1990). The core competence of the corporation. *Harvard Business Review, 90*(3), 79–91.

Prietula, M. J., & Simon, H. A. (1989). The experts in your midst. *Harvard Business Review, 67*(1), 120–124.

Raelin, J. A. (1984a). The salaried professional: How to make the most of your career. New York: Praeger.

Raelin, J. A. (1984b). An examination of deviant/adaptive behaviors in the organizational careers of professionals. *Academy of Management Review, 9*(3), 413–427.

Ranftl, R. M. (1977). Improving R&D productivity: A study program and its application. *Research Management, 20*(1), 25–29.

Ritti, R. R. (1971). Dual management—Does it work? *Research Management, 14*(5), 19–26.

Roseman, E. (1977). *Confronting nonpromotability.* New York: AMACOM.

Rosen, N., Billings, R., & Turney, J. (1976). The emergence and allocation of leadership resources over time in a technical organization. *Academy of Management Journal, 19*(2), 165–182.

Rosenbaum, J. E. (1979). Tournament mobility: Career patterns in a corporation. *Administrative Science Quarterly, 24*(2), 221–241.

Rothman, R. A., & Perrucci, R. (1970). Organizational careers and professional expertise. *Administrative Science Quarterly, 15*(3), 282–294.

Sarason, S. B. (1977). *Work, aging, and social change.* New York: The Free Press.

Savage, P. L., & Gabriel, R. A. (1980). Turning away from managerialism: The environment of military leadership. *Military Review*, U.S. Army Command and General Staff College, Fort Leavenworth, KS.

Schein, E. H. (1977). Career anchors and career paths: A panel study of management school graduates. In J. Van Maanen (Ed.), *Organizational careers: Some new perspectives*, (pp. 3–22). London: Wiley.

Schien, E. H. (1982). Increasing organizational effectiveness through better human resource planning and development. In R. Katz (Ed.), *Career issues in human resource development* (pp. 3–32). Englewood Cliffs, NJ: Prentice-Hall.

Scholl, R. W. (1983). Career lines and employment stability. *Academy of Management Journal, 26*(1), 86–103.

Schroeter, D. G. (1977). Success and failure. *Research Management, 20*(4), 31–32.

Shapero, A. (1983, November-December). Keeping R&D professionals alive. *Research Management*, pp. 7–8.

Shapero, A. (1985). *Managing Professional People.* New York: The Free Press.

Smith, J. J., & Szabo, T. T. (1977). Importance of flexibility, job content and individual temperament. *Research Management, XX*(4), 20–23.

Thompson, P. H., & Dalton, G. W. (1976). Are R&D organizations obsolete? *Harvard Business Review, 54*(6), 105–116.

Van Maanen, J. (1982). Boundary crossings: Major strategies of organizational socialization and their consequences. In R. Katz (Ed.), *Career issues in human resource management* (pp. 85–115). Englewood Cliffs, NJ: Prentice-Hall.

Vardi, Y. (1980). Organizational career mobility: An integrative model. *Academy of Management Review, 5*(3), 341–355.

Veiga, J. F. (1981a). Do managers on the move get anywhere? *Harvard Business, 5*(2), 20–22, 26–30, 34–38.

Veiga, J. F. (1981b). Plateaued versus nonplateaued managers: Career patterns, attitudes, and path potential. *Academy of Management Journal, 24*(3), 566–578.

Veiga, J. F. (1983). Mobility influences during managerial career stages. *Academy of Management Journal, 26*(1), 64–85.

Von Glinow, M. A., Driver, M. J., Brousseau, K., & Prince, J. B. (1983). The design of a career oriented human resource system. *Academy of Management Review, 8*(1), 23–32.

5

Career Transitions
in Changing Times

Frank J. Minor
Saint Anselm College

L. Allen Slade
Ford Motor Company

Roger A. Myers
Teachers College, Columbia University

Career transitions are normal and expected aspects of an employee's career development. However, the rate of change in business strategies and organizational structure, and the frequency of acquisitions have increased the probability that employees will experience disruptive career transitions. Such changes could include geographical relocation, transfer, demotion, or being sidetracked into a deadend and plateauing position.

All career transitions create role ambiguities, risks, and exposures for employees that often result in perceptions of a loss of control and stress. Role ambiguities are characterized by uncertainty about one's responsibilities, peer relationships, mission, and career path. Risks that may need to be dealt with include financial exposures from salary reductions, financing the cost of a new house, cost-of-living increases, spouse's job loss, and loss of employment security. In today's business environment many employees are faced with these types of scenarios. Stress resulting from such situations may manifest itself at a psychological level by causing anxiety, loss of self-esteem, and job dissatisfaction. At the behavioral level the consequences to the individual and the organization could include diminished performance, absenteeism, increased use of grievance channels, and turnover. At the physiological level the employee's health may be at risk, possibly resulting in illness and fatigue.

Models have been created for ease of description of cause and effect relationships of the factors involved and the coping strategies adopted by individuals experiencing a job or career disruption. An example is presented in Fig. 5.1 (Knicki, 1989). According to the model, employee perception of the importance of different kinds of stressors, or stress inducing forces, can vary as a function of employee personal background factors. More highly trained or educated employees, for example, might be less stressed by relocation than their counterparts because the former are probably better equipped with the knowledge and skills needed to deal with the uncertainties of a new job. Employees' personal resources that can be drawn on include their social contacts, performance potential, and personality traits. Persons with a high self-esteem, or those who are self-directed (i.e., have an internal locus of control), are more likely to engage in active problem-solving coping behaviors. Similarly, high performers would enter into a career transition with self-confidence conducive to a problem-solving strategy.

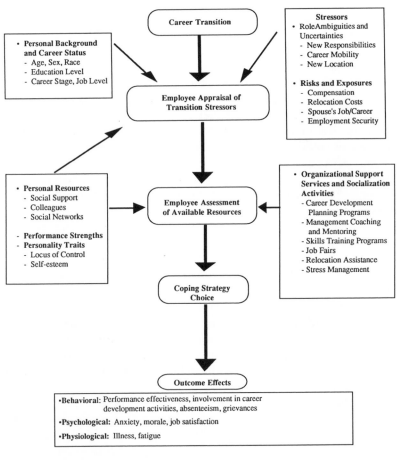

FIG. 5.1. Career transition adaptation process.

Organizational support resources that might be drawn on by employees in career transitions include career development planning programs, internal job skills training courses, job fairs that precede redeployment actions, stress management training, relocation assistance programs, and timely manager–employee performance planning sessions for new job assignments.

IMPACT OF CAREER TRANSITIONS ON EMPLOYEES

During the career transition process the disruptions of established behaviors and the stress created by uncertainty interfere with the employee's job performance. However, as employees adapt to their new roles, increases in innovative contributions and personal growth will be realized. As used here, innovation is not limited to the discovery or introduction of technological or methods improvements. Rather, innovation includes all forms of organizational role development that Brett (1984) defined as "job behaviors exhibited by the new role incumbent that were not engaged in by the previous role incumbent" (p. 156). Innovation therefore, can embrace behaviors as diverse as a new sales person's attention to a different set of clientele, a new computer programmer's redesign of system data files, and a new executive's reorganization of a department.

Schein (1971) contrasted the relative degrees to which employees engage in innovative and socialization behavior during a career transition. *Socialization* is defined as the activities engaged in by employees in order to learn how they fit into the context of their new job in terms of tasks, interpersonal relationships, performance criteria, the reward system, and future career growth opportunities (Katz, 1984; Schein, 1978). Socialization activities increase immediately before and after a career transition as employees adapt to their new role. Innovative behavior is greatest between career transitions, that is, after the employee's adaptation to the new role and before preparations begin for the next career transition. If the transitions follow one another too rapidly, the investment in the socialization process may lessen the potential for innovative behavior.

The ease of adjustment and the time required by employees to reach their full potential following a transition is related to the compatibility between the new job, career plans, skills, and expectations about the new job. The greater the compatibility, the less time required to achieve full performance potential (Brett & Werbel, 1980). The new manager of an employee involved in a transition can strongly influence the adaptation process. Managers should avoid a "sink or swim" leadership style with employees who have just transferred to their department. Instead, managers should provide on-the-job coaching that initially favors a directive approach during the transition period. In addition, employees benefit from frequent performance assessment, feedback, and rewards provided by their manager immediately following a job or career change. Given the manager's central role in the adaptation process, increased interpersonal contact between managers and their employees can help employees more effectively cope with their career transitions (Pascale, 1985).

In some cases, employees may be asked to make a career transition in order to support an organization's efforts to streamline its structure or to enhance productivity. Such transitions can be thought of as supporting *organizational role development*. Role development can be realized by filling a position with a person known for behaviors needed in the position that were not performed by previous incumbents. The conditions needed for role development, according to Brett (1984), are quite different from those needed for employee personal development. Personal development is most likely to occur when individuals encounter new work experiences, are assigned specific job goals, and receive rich personal performance feedback. Organizational role development, on the other hand, is maximized when the individuals are not required to learn new skills, and are not dependent on high levels of performance feedback. In the case of role development, the transition issue is the shaping of the job, not how the job can shape the employee's personal qualifications.

Behavioral processes common to transitions have been discussed earlier. In spite of many common features, different types of career transitions can present different problems to employees. The unique aspects of three transitions—relocation, demotion, and plateauing—are described below.

Geographic Relocation. Geographic relocation involves an abrupt environmental change for the employee and the family as well as a work role change for the employee. Approximately 800,000 heads of households are annually relocated by their employers (Sell, 1983). In some cases, employees are requested to relocate as part of a group in order to consolidate several different operating units, redeploy surplus skill groups, or to phase out an unnecessary operation. Group moves usually are not perceived as an attractive transition by employees because they often are requested to do the same kind of work for the same pay, but at a different location.

Conversely, when an individual is offered a geographic relocation it is more often for reasons of the individual's personal development as well as to satisfy an organizational need. These relocations can involve a promotion, a transfer to acquire new work experiences, or an assignment to provide the organization with specific expertise at a new site.

Research studies have investigated variables contributing to employees' expression of willingness to relocate, acceptance or rejection of a relocation offer, satisfaction with a move, and personal adjustment after relocation.

Studies of expressed willingness consistently indicate that the major factors that reduce mobility are family resistance (especially when teenagers have strong school ties or the spouse is employed), increasing age of the employee and spouse, the perception that the new job is not a positive career development step, community ties, financial risks associated with the cost of the move (such as the cost of living and mortgage interest rates), and a lack of prior relocation experience (Brett, 1981; Domsch, Kruger, & Gerpott, 1984; Howard & Bray, 1980).

Studies in which actual relocation offers are presented to employees indicate that the range of acceptance rates varies as a function of career development and promotion opportunities associated with the move, the employee's job level, the skill group or occupational group of which the employee is a member, and various personal and family demographic characteristics (Brett, 1981; Minor, 1981). In general, employees who accept relocation offers do so because they perceive the job offer to be challenging and to be a positive career step. The weight of the factors that contribute to the decision to accept or refuse a relocation offers varies significantly amongst managers, nonmanagerial professionals, and nonexempt employees. Managers are most influenced by job/career and salary factors, whereas nonmanagerial employees are influenced by a wide range of factors that include their spouse's career, perceptions about quality of life in the present versus the proposed location, financial risks (such as the cost of living and mortgage rates), and social ties (Minor, 1981). Younger employees and those in marketing and sales are more likely to accept a relocation than their counterparts (Brett, 1981; Minor, 1981).

Once the relocation takes place, there are a number of activities that contribute to the personal adjustment of the family and employees' adjustment to their new job. Personal adjustment is affected by the spouse's success in becoming reemployed at the new location, selling or buying a house, moving expense reimbursement, establishing ties in the new community and the children's adjustment to school and peers (Brett & Werbel, 1980; Minor, 1981; Pinder, 1977, 1978). In the long run, the compensation received for the new job is critical to the employee's later expressed satisfaction with the move (Pinder, 1978).

The time required for on-the-job adjustment is highly related to the correspondence between the actual job duties and responsibilities and those initially described to the transferee (Minor, 1981). Relocations that are anticipated in advance and involve only a moderate change in level or function are the easiest because of the carry over from the old job (Brett & Werbel, 1980). An example of a difficult transition would be the redeploying of salaried technical workers from laboratories into field sales positions for which pay is based on sales quotas.

A short demanding orientation following a relocation often results in more rapid job adjustment than a prolonged leisurely orientation (Bateman, Karwan, & Kazee, 1983).

A key question is whether the disruptions and stress of a mobile lifestyle have an adverse effect on the well-being of employees, their spouses, and their children. There are few differences in satisfaction between geographically mobile people and less mobile, stable people. Mobile employees indicated greater satisfaction with their lives than did less mobile employees, but did show decreased satisfaction with their social relationships (Brett, 1982).

There are a number of implications for management practices based on the research cited. In order to provide a positive employee attitude toward mobility and to assure that employees make the best decision regarding a relocation offer, the responsible managers should:

- Be certain that transfers are compatible with and supportive of the employees' career development plans
- Clearly define the new job in terms of its content, challenge, and its career growth implications
- Provide early involvement by the employees' spouses through survey trips to the proposed location for the purpose of exploring community characteristics and job opportunities
- Provide employees with information about the financial implications of the move in terms of a cash flow analysis dealing with taxes, mortgage, housing prices, and salary.

Although the subject of employee relocation has been highly researched, conversely there is very little research information available for the next type of career transition discussed, demotion.

Demotion. Demotion can be a part of an effective human resource strategy that combines employment security with uncertainty of position security (Goldner, 1965). With this strategy, employees who perform inadequately are demoted rather than dismissed from the organization. The possibility of demotion motivates employees to pursue excellence, whereas employment security gives a sense of stability needed to take appropriate business risks. When the potential for demotion exists, employees become aware that they must take some risks to succeed and sustain their level in the organization. They accept the possibility of failure and demotion because they have employment security. In contrast, if the organization fires employees for reason of failure, employees will avoid responsibilities that involve risky decisions.

There are several ways an organization can make demotion less traumatic for the employee. One method is by "cloaking" the demotion (Goldner, 1965). Cloaking can be accomplished in several ways. If the lines of organizational authority are kept vague, it is often unclear whether a job move is up, down, or lateral. Also, the use of special job or training assignments can obscure a demotion. Geographic relocation can also make a demotion more acceptable by providing the individual with a new set of co-workers as opposed to cloaking the demotion at the current location. Another way an organization can ease the adjustment to a demotion is by fostering "zig-zag mobility," so that demoted employees can later be promoted if their job performance warrants it (Goldner, 1965). Zig-zag mobility can be contrasted with "tournament mobility" (Rosenbaum, 1979), in which failure in an early part of a career limits the individual's chance for promotion later.

Of interest is the observation that awareness of the potential for a demotion may enhance organizational effectiveness. Nondemoted managers demonstrated an improvement in their performance following the demotion of other executives ("Organization & performance," 1983). Two-way communication was unexpectedly enhanced after demotions were implemented, apparently because demoted individuals acted as communication links between the surviving managers and their subordinates (Hall, 1976).

To make downward moves more positive for the employee and the organization, organizations should involve the employee in the new job choice, have the new job demand the learning of new skills so that it is a growth move, counsel the employee about future options, provide life and career planning workshops, sustain the employee's current salary, and place the employee in a new physical and social setting (Hall & Isabella, 1986).

Plateauing. Plateauing is included in this discussion of transitions because it is a form of career transition that involves a change in job mobility expectations. Plateauing is often triggered by a "nonevent" such as an expected promotion that does not occur (Schlossberg, 1981). In the case of organizational change such as restructuring, change in technology, or downsizing, employees may suddenly realize that their career path or career mobility has been abruptly blocked. As with geographic relocation, promotion, or demotion, plateaued individuals must reassess their role in the organization. This reassessment leads to a transition requiring a period of personal adaptation to new expectations. Plateauing is a unique form of career transition because there may be no change in tasks that can cause task-related ambiguity. Also, although some career transitions have a very distinct point of transition, plateauing may involve only a gradual change in mobility expectations. This leads to an ambiguous boundary for the plateau transition. A good example of a distinct point of transition would be in the military services. In the Navy, whether an officer is plateaued or not is clearly known not only to the officer, but also to his or her peers on the day it occurs. Chances for an officer's promotion will go from 55% to 90% on one day; down to 3% to 5% the next. Despite the uniqueness of plateauing, many of the psychological processes involved in other more abrupt career transitions apply to plateauing.

Some form of plateauing is ultimately faced by all employees. Plateaued employees are of concern to organizations because of the potential consequences to motivation and performance. Plateaued employees have been characterized as *shelf-sitters* (Connor & Fielden, 1973), suggesting that they become relatively inactive after becoming plateaued. Reductions in the mobility expectations of employees can have an adverse effect on their work behavior (Goldner, 1965).

There are several types of plateauing that should be differentiated. The first distinction to be made is the impact of plateauing on expectations of future job changes. *Structural plateauing* occurs if there is no expectation of future promotion because of the limited number of positions available at higher levels. This type of plateauing is becoming more common because of reduced growth and downsizing of middle management positions in organizations (Spruell, 1985). *Content plateauing* occurs when there is no expectation of new job challenges or variation in job duties. Because of the pyramidal structure of most organizations, structural plateauing is virtually inevitable (Bardwick, 1984). Yet, a person who is structurally plateaued does not have to be content plateaued. Lateral transfers or changes in specific job duties can provide continuing challenges and new experiences for those who do not expect further promotions (Spruell, 1985).

A second distinction should be made in terms of the performance of the plateaued employees. *Deadwood* are low-performing plateaued employees. In contrast, *solid citizens* are plateaued but maintain a high level of performance. Solid citizens are central to the organization's effective functioning because they often compose a large part of the more tenured management group and provide stability to the organization (Ference, Stoner, & Warren, 1977). Several studies have investigated employee reactions to career plateauing. In a longitudinal study, Howard and Bray (1980) found that "most managers had accepted their career plateaus and adjusted to them" (p. 5). Only 10% of another group of managers were concerned about plateauing, and this percentage decreased with age (Tausky & Dubin, 1965). Structural plateauing appears to be relatively well accepted by most individuals. In the Navy example cited earlier, even though plateaued officers tend to be sidetracked or put in limbo, their commitment and satisfaction with the Navy is not significantly different from officers who are promoted (Morrison & Wilcove, 1985).

Several management practices can help minimize the potential for loss of motivation due to plateauing. First, individuals should be prepared for plateauing. Structural plateauing requires that the phenomenon be clearly communicated in order to maintain acceptance by organizational members (Kelly, 1985). As part of the hiring process, a realistic job preview (Wanous, 1975) should include an appraisal of the opportunities for promotion and highlight the eventuality of structural plateauing. Career development planning sessions should communicate that plateauing is an expected stage of the employee's career (Christiansen, 1983). Such development planning sessions should not focus on preparation for promotion, but rather on skills development planning and enhancement of flexibility in preparation for future opportunities and new development avenues.

Second, plateaued employees with different levels of performance should be managed differently (Odiorne, 1984). Deadwood employees should be managed as poor performers. The manager should review behavioral deficiencies with poor performing employees, plan remedial activities to address deficiencies, and set performance goals within the context of a measurable assignment. If performance does not improve, the manager should consider demotion, retraining, or separation of the individuals from the company.

Solid citizens require a different type of management attention. Management tends to ignore solid citizens (Ference et al., 1977) because their continued high performance causes no crisis. This tendency increases the likelihood that solid citizens will ultimately become deadwood. To avoid this, solid citizens should be provided with career development planning services, special job assignments, and skills training, which will provide opportunities for intellectual and motivational revitalization (Ference et al., 1977). Finally, organizations should consider career-long job rotation in order to prevent content plateauing (Ference et al., 1977; Hall 1976). An expectation of new job challenges and opportunities for personal growth can help prevent the solid citizen from becoming deadwood. One drawback of career-long job rotations is that it increases the number of career transitions in the organization and thereby increases the need for the organization to actively manage the transitions.

CONCLUSIONS

Organizations can take several actions to increase employee receptivity and adaptability to career transitions, and to sustain their commitment to continued development within the organization (Gaertner, 1988). First, the organization should communicate its commitment to on-going development and utilization of its internal work force as a means of meeting its changing business demands. Second, management must forecast the organization's changing skills demands and shifts in the numbers of employees needed in different types of jobs. This information must be communicated to employees by means of the organization's career planning programs so their personal development planning can be responsive to organizational change. Third, the organization's career planning program should enable employees to relate their personal attributes to a wide range of development avenues so they can discover their multipotentiality within the organization and identify career path options. Gaertner (1988) recommended that organizations increase the flexibility of career paths by making only tentative decisions about the placement of individuals and providing them with the opportunity to have several short-term career assignments in different parts of the organization. These short careers could last several years in each of several functions and would produce a versatile and flexible talent pool to accommodate the organization's changing business needs. For such a career planning program to succeed, however, employees must be empowered to make their own choices from the opportunities available and must perceive that management is committed to their ongoing personal growth and development.

REFERENCES

Bardwick, J. M. (1984). When ambition is no asset. *New Management, 1*(4), 22–28.

Bateman, J. S., Karwan, K. R., & Kazee, T. A. (1983) Getting a fresh start: A natural quasi-experimental test of the performance effects of moving to a new job. *Journal of Applied Psychology, 68*, 517–524.

Brett, J. M. (1981, August). *Employee transfers. The effects of job transfers on employees and their families.* Paper presented at the annual meeting of the Academy of Management, San Diego, CA.

Brett, J. M. (1982). Job transfer and well-being. *Journal of Applied Psychology, 67*, 450–463.

Brett, J. M. (1984). Job transitions and personal and role development. In K. M. Rowland & G. Ferris (Eds.), *Research in personnel and human resources management* (Vol. 2, pp. 155–185). Greenwich, CT: JAI Press.

Brett, J. M., & Werbel, J. D. (1980). *The effect of job transfer on employees and their families* (Research Report) Washington, DC: Employee Relocation Council.

Christiansen, K. C., (1983, August). *Case study of a career management system.* Paper presented at the annual meeting of the American Psychological Association, Anaheim, CA.

Connor, S. R., & Fielden, J. S. (1973, November-December). Rx for managerial 'shelf-sitters'. *Harvard Business Review*, pp. 113–120.

Domsch, M., Kruger, M., & Gerpott, T. J. (1984, August). *General propensity to be geographically mobile across family life cycle.* Paper presented at the meeting of the Academy of Management, Boston, MA.

Ference, T. P., Stoner, J. A. F., & Warren, E. K. (1977). Managing the career plateau. *Academy of Management Review, 2*, 602–612.

Gaertner, K. N. (1988), Managers' careers and organizational change. *Academy of Management Executive, 11*(4), 311–318.

Goldner, F. H. (1965). Demotion in industrial management. *American Sociological Review, 30*, 714–724.

Hall, D. T. (1976). *Careers in organizations.* Dallas: Scott, Foresman.

Hall, D. T., & Isabella, L. A. (1986). Downward moves: Alternative career development. *The*

Career Center Bulletin, 5, 6–7.

Howard, A., & Bray, D. W. (1980, September). *Career motivation in mid-life managers.* Paper presented at the annual American Psychological Association Conference, Montreal, Canada.

Katz, R. (1984). Organizational stress and early socialization experiences. In T. Beehr & R. Bhagat (Eds.), *Human stress and cognitions in organization: An integrative perspective* (pp. 117–139). New York: Wiley.

Kelly, J. F. (1985). Coping with the career plateau. *Personnel Administrator, 30,* 65–76.

Kinicki, A., (1989, April). *Job loss and stress.* Paper presented at the conference of the Society for Industrial and Organizational Psychology, Boston.

Minor, F. J. (1981, August). *Employee relocation mobility study.* Paper presented at the 41st annual meeting of the Academy of Management, San Diego, CA.

Morrison, R. F., & Wilcove, G. L. (1985, August). *Career plateaued managers and the selection-adjustment controversy.* Paper presented at the annual meeting of the Academy of Management, San Diego.

Odiorne, G. S. (1984). *Strategic management of human resources.* San Francisco: Jossey-Bass.

Organization and performance (1983, August). *Rydge's,* pp. 82–85.

Pascale, R. (1985, Winter). The paradox of corporate culture. Recruiting ourselves to socialization. *California Management Review,* p. 27.

Pinder, C. C. (1977). Multiple predictors of post-transfer satisfaction: The role of urban factors. *Personnel Psychology, 30,* 543–556.

Pinder, C. C. (1978). Corporate transfer policy: Comparative reactions of managers and their spouses. *Relations Industrielles, 33,* 654–665.

Rosenbaum, J. E. (1979). Tournament mobility: Career patterns in a corporation. *Administrative Science Quarterly, 24,* 220–241.

Schein, E. H. (1971). The individual, the organization, and the career: A conceptual scheme. *Journal of Applied Science, 4,* 401–426.

Schein, E. H. (1978). *Career dynamics: Matching individual and organizational needs.* Reading, MA: Addison-Wesley.

Schlossberg, N. K. (1981). A model for analyzing human adaptation to transition. *The Counseling Psychologist, 9* (2), 2–18.

Sell, R. R. (1983). Transferred jobs: A neglected aspect of migration and occupational change. *Work and Occupations, 10,* 179–206.

Spruell, G. (1985). Say so long to promotions. *Training & Development Journal, 39,* 70–75.

Tausky, C. T., & Dubin, R. (1965). Career anchorage: Managerial mobility motivations. *American Sociological Review, 30,* 725–735.

Wanous, J. P. (1975). Tell it like it is at realistic job previews. *Personnel, 52,* 50–60.

6

Career Decision Making

Nancy Hicks
Rutgers University

Manuel London
State University of New York-Stony Brook

Career decisions come in all shapes and sizes. Some are of major importance to us, such as the choice of an occupation, the decision to quit one job and accept another, and the decision to retire. Other career decisions are less momentous, such as the decision to transfer jobs within the same organization and the decision to behave differently, thereby changing one's role in the organization. Some career decisions mean great changes in our lives, and others do not. Some career decisions affect our families, and must be made with them, or at least with them in mind. In fact, a career decision may be brought about because of nonwork concerns, such as the need to make more money to send children to college or the need to change jobs because one's spouse is being transferred.

Obviously, career decisions are not simple. There are many different types, and they happen throughout our careers. Career decisions occur within the context of a complex life space influenced by individual characteristics, organizational circumstances, and conditions outside the organization. Career decisions are usually treated in the literature as situationally specific and static in nature. This means that the focus is usually on a single decision, such as "What field should I go into?" But when viewed as an interrelated series of role changes over time, career decisions take on broader significance as a way of understanding and affecting what happens in our careers.

This chapter examines how we make career decisions, factors affecting decision processes, and actions people and organizations take to help make career decisions. By applying theory and research in the general areas of decision making and career dynamics, we offer a practical perspective to guide organizational programs and policies that influence career decisions.

We do not attempt to provide an exhaustive review of the literature. Nor do we offer a comprehensive model of career decisions (see Mihal, Sorce, & Comte, 1984; Phillips & Pazienza, 1988, for descriptions of such models). Rather, we highlight central aspects of career decision making. We view career decision making as a dynamic, on-going process that fits into a developmental view of careers. We view a career as a sequence of roles and transitions (Hall, 1976). Our model is integrative, suggesting how different psychological processes work together under different conditions. Moreover, we try to show leverage points for impacting career decisions. This leads us to examples of organizational policies and programs and individual initiatives to influence career decisions for the good of the individual and the organization.

The topics of the chapter are outlined in Fig. 6.1. The chapter begins with a description of different types of career decisions at different career stages. We consider factors that precipitate these decisions, recognizing that sometimes the need to make a decision occurs deliberately, initiated by the individual, and at other times the decision is at the mercy of current opportunities and chance. We review how people evaluate their circumstances using both a prospective view that looks into the future, and a retrospective view that looks backward and allows us to rationalize our actions. We then turn to how people make decisions. This discussion covers prescriptive, optimizing approaches ("the best way") as well as the more descriptive, satisficing approaches ("making do"). We argue that part of the decision process is how we commit ourselves to career decisions and the impact of existing commitments on our decisions. This leads to a discussion of organizational factors and individual characteristics affecting the decisions we have to make and how we make them. We conclude with a review of organizational programs and individual actions for facilitating career decision making.

TYPES OF CAREER DECISIONS:
A DEVELOPMENTAL PERSPECTIVE

There is no set time or age for many of the events that can occur in our lives and the decisions we may face. Nevertheless, a convenient way to organize types of career decisions is according to career and life stages. This places career decisions within a developmental perspective. First, we consider the impact of life stages on career decisions. Next we turn to the meaning and influence of career stages, and then we examine career decisions in the form of role changes and adjustments.

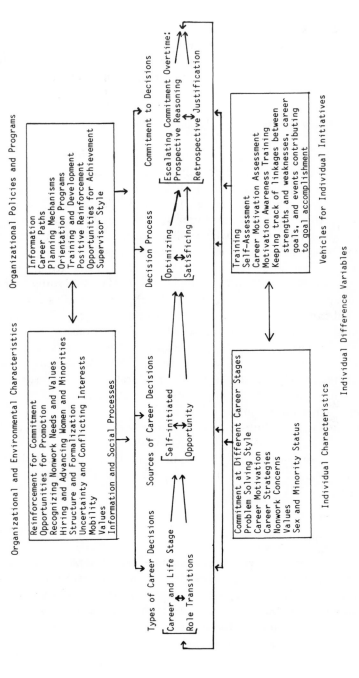

FIG. 6.1. Variables influencing career decisions.

123

Life Stages and Transitions

Consider a simplified view of adulthood from the time we usually start our careers—a view that focuses on important life transitions (Levinson, 1977). The early adulthood transition, typically between the ages of 17 and 22, is the time when we make initial career choices. The age-30 transition, between 28 and 33, may be a time for occupational change. The transition from early to middle adulthood, between 35 and 45, may be a time of questioning one's established life structure, a time of crisis that is the impetus for career change. Later life stages continue to involve changes in career and life roles, including retirement.

At mid-life both men and women start to view their lives in terms of the time left until death rather than the time elapsed (Neugarten, 1976). This and other predictable changes in perspective have their effect on the individual's thinking regarding his or her career. Less predictable events, such as divorce or the death of a child upset the sequence of the life cycle and may bring about crisis behavior, the impact of which will have a decidedly different flavor from the more "normative" developmental happenings.

How we view ourselves, our "ego identity," is tied to career and life development (Brown, Brooks, & associates, 1984). According to this view, age-related crises must be resolved at the appropriate life stage before the individual can go on to the next period of development. Throughout life, individuals form and reform their sense of self in response to crises as well as to other life experiences. This process affects the person's career decision making. In making a career choice, the decision maker moves through a series of steps that lead from the initial consideration of a choice to a new state of integration, in which people reorganize both themselves and the environment. Thus, the evolution of ego identity is a psychological process that corresponds to and at times is synonymous with individual career decision making. For instance, a young woman joins the armed forces and becomes an officer. Her identity is slowly tied to being in the military and distinct from life as a civilian. Consequently, leaving the military would be a wrenching experience.

Career Stages

We can distinguish between three sequential career stages people experience in an organizational setting: (a) establishment (the first year), (b) advancement (Years 2–4), and (c) maintenance (Year 5 and beyond) (Hall & Nougaim, 1968; Super, 1957). The first is characterized by skill building and competency development, the second by upward mobility, and the last by leveling off and reduction of competition.

Career stages may be interpreted in terms of the career decisions we face. The early years after choosing an occupation and a first job are a time for evaluation and decisions about sticking with it or moving on to another job or perhaps to a different occupation. This is a period of initiating career goals and plans, which is also a type of career decision. Mid-career is often a time of re-assessment of our career goals in light of career progress. This may result in drastic changes (the infamous "mid-career change") or simply adjustment or affirmation of our career goals.

The concepts of life and career stages help us understand individuals' career decisions at various points in their lives and help distinguish between different types of responses to career outcomes. However, organizational experiences and opportunities (described later) influence the decisions one faces and one's reactions. This may cause the individual to recycle through establishment, advancement, and maintenance career stages, contrary to the fixed, age-bound paradigm implied by Levinson's work.

Role Transitions as Career Decisions

A career change may be *interrole* (moving to a new work role) or *intrarole* (adopting a new orientation to an old work role) (Louis, 1980a). Possible career transitions initiated by the individual include promotion, transfer, a new job within the company or in another company, early retirement, and retirement. Other examples are requesting and accepting a new assignment or added responsibilities, adopting a new attitude toward an old job, or making a change in a nonwork role, such as starting a family, which leads to a change in a work role.

Responses to new roles may be interpreted as types of career decisions. Employees may assume a new attitude toward an old job by modifying themselves to meet the job demands, modifying the work role to meet personal demands, or a combination of the two (Nicholson, 1984). Adjustments occur as employees occupy a role for longer periods of time. An individual may begin by learning the job requirements and then move through periods of accepting, evaluating, and redefining the work role.

Thus, career decisions may be viewed broadly in terms of discrete decisions that lead to a major transition in one's career and life in general. Also, career decisions may be viewed as part of the transition process as we adapt to and create work roles. Our point is not that all work behaviors entail some type of career decision, however small, but rather that career decisions are tied together and form the basis for many of the roles we play. Moreover, career decisions are affected by our current roles. Thus, career decision making is an on-going process. From a practical standpoint, however, it makes sense to concentrate on the important career decisions, especially those involving job changes. The next section considers how the need to make such a career decision arises.

SELF-INITIATED AND OPPORTUNITY-DRIVEN CAREER DECISIONS

Thinking Ahead

One view of career decisions is that they arise from a felt discrepancy between current career roles and role expectations. According to this prospective approach, employees initiate a sequence of problem recognition, strategy formation, information search, evaluation, and choice. This sequence of events assumes that the choice process is orderly and based on the desire to resolve the feeling of dissatisfaction. (We return to the discussion of a career decision as an orderly process later.)

Some career decisions, however, do not arise as a result of a discrepancy perceived by individuals. Instead, they are the response to opportunities presented to them. For instance, incentive packages for early retirement may be offered by a company to reduce surplus employees. Most companies extend promotions without being solicited by targeted employees to do so. Other organizations such as the military tender promotions on a somewhat regular basis.

An Opportunity-Based Model

Many people have different careers than they envisioned when they graduated from school (Roberts, 1968). Over time, they develop ambitions consistent with the jobs they hold. "Popular common sense conceives individuals as making up their minds about the sort of work they wish to do, and then selecting appropriate jobs," yet "the typical pattern of interaction seems not to be for jobs to be entered upon the basis of ambitions, but for ambitions to be adapted to the occupations that young people find themselves able to enter" (Roberts, 1968, p. 174).

Graduating high school students tend to make career decisions based on the opportunities open to them (Rothstein, 1980). If the family is able to afford college and a college offered a chance for them to attend, the students go to college. When jobs are in high supply, students may leave school for jobs. When the job market is tight, they stay in school or join the military.

For those in college or entering the job market, the most common experience is not to obtain a job that closely matches one's career expectations or goals, but to reorganize attitudes, goals, or concepts so as to increase the congruence between one's self-concept or self-expectation and the selected occupation's potential for fulfilling these expectations (Brown, 1970).

Most careers are "a series of responses to a succession of opportunity situations [rather] than the effort to realize a predetermined occupational goal" (Rothstein, 1980, p. 328). An *opportunity structure model* accounts for career progression. Once our career expectations are brought into line with the occupations we find ourselves able to enter, the opportunity structure opened up by the nature of the early job accounts for our later career development. That is, where we are at any given time influences the opportunities open to us.

In the organizational context, the opportunity structure model helps explain employee retention. Once new hires enter the organization and become committed to it, they are likely to remain if opportunities regularly present themselves within the organization. Proximity is an important part of this model. When sufficiently attractive opportunities outside the organization become apparent, the individual's career may move in the direction of these opportunities instead of remaining within the organization.

The opportunities that influence career decisions are not just job opportunities. People use other choice situations, such as the decision to marry or to divorce, as occasions to make career decisions. Individuals do not have single goals, but they have multiple goals that often conflict or that they try to satisfy simultaneously (Rothstein, 1980). The presentation of an opportunity can produce an impasse, or can resolve an impasse created by multiple goals. The decision procedure used to support such career choices has been called a process of *successive limited comparisons*. Each opportunity situation permits the individual to correct previous errors and take new goals into consideration.

Some opportunities are more "surprising" than others in that they are expected to a greater or lesser degree by the decision maker (Louis, 1980b). Although employees in highly structured organizations may come to expect promotions within certain periods of time, others will be confronted with unexpected opportunities.

Retrospective reasoning often accompanies the acceptance of an opportunity. "Once a choice has been made, the behavioral act may serve as a constraining reality that can shape future attitudes and behavior" (O'Reilly & Caldwell, 1981, p. 597). Individuals make sense of their choices by creating acceptable justifications for them. Such sense-making activity may occur prior to or following the acceptance of a decision opportunity, but in either case, the rationalizing character of the reasoning process is similar. Individuals accommodate their acts and their attitudes to the choices they make. This does not preclude the possibility that some objective data will be used in the process of accommodation.

The aforementioned explains how people starting their-careers are able to bring their ambitions into line with the occupations they are able to enter. It also raises the possibility that different career decisions may be made in different ways. The kind of process used, whether prospective or opportunity-based, may depend on individual cognitive differences, training, context, whether an individual or an organization initiates the decision, whether an attractive opportunity has presented itself, whether an employee is satisfied with his or her present position, and nonwork factors as well.

An Integrative Decision-Making Model

A career decision-making model should take into account both opportunity-initiated and prospective decision making. Such a model needs to be a process model that depicts career decision making as an ongoing process that does not cease once one decision has been made. Career decision making may require an intentional, prospective decision-making sequence, even when that sequence is initiated by an opportunity. However, long-lasting career decisions have at times been made impulsively in response to the serendipitous appearance of an unsought opportunity.

That many career decisions are essential responses to organizationally initiated opportunities is not necessarily negative. Sometimes organizations have a more objective view of the individual's capabilities than the individual does. And simply because an employee accepts an organizationally initiated opportunity does not mean that he or she has not gone through a careful decision sequence before accepting the opportunity. Finally, a proffered opportunity may be the result of a well-organized search-and-choose process, and as such reflects a minimum of rationalizing and justifying.

In summary, a career decision process may be precipitated either by a perceived discrepancy between the present situation and the employee's career expectations, by an opportunity offered to the employee, or both. An opportunity may create a felt discrepancy, and a felt discrepancy causes one to seek opportunities. We discussed prospective reasoning as the sequential, logical process that is initiated when a discrepancy is felt. We also discussed retrospective reasoning as a way of justifying our responses to events that are beyond our control but that present opportunities. We should note that career decisions can lead to no changes. Career decisions deal not only with organizational opportunities but also with the rejection of organizational opportunities and the seeking of new options. The following section considers the choice process in more depth.

HOW PEOPLE MAKE CAREER DECISIONS: OPTIMIZING VERSUS SATISFICING

Optimizing

Optimizing implies choosing the best alternative from among all relevant alternatives. The process begins with a thorough exploration of the environment and identification of alternatives followed by in-depth evaluation of each alternative, and the selection of the best alternative. This is a prospective, forward-looking process. It is also unrealistic. More likely, career decisions are made using combinations of prospective and retrospective reasoning.

Satisficing

To understand how prospective and retrospective reasoning work together, consider the example of a person who perceives a discrepancy between his or her career goals and the present situation. A prospective process is initiated and the individual begins to gather information over a period of time, only to suddenly face an unexpected opportunity. Although the individual has not gathered enough information to adequately weigh the opportunity against other alternatives, it appears to be "good enough," and so it is accepted. The individual then makes further sense of the choice by justifying it via his or her characteristic cognitive style, past experience, and prevailing organizational values.

This combined prospective, opportunity-based decision process might be described as *satisficing*. Using a satisficing strategy, the decision maker may go with the first appropriate alternative. The assumption is that the decision maker has formally or informally set a minimum level of acceptability. In contrast, in an optimizing strategy more descriptive of purely prospective rationality, the decision maker selects the best alternative among all those available (Simon, 1976).

Contingency Models for Decision Making

There is no reason to believe that all career decisions are made in the same manner. Different kinds of situations may call for particular decision strategies. These are contingency models for decision making in which the demands of the task determine the strategies chosen by the individual.

For instance, as the number of possible choices increases, the tendency to use an optimizing decision strategy decreases (Payne, 1976). In using an optimizing strategy to choose between two alternatives, the decision maker will often go through a process of "trading-off between a high value of one dimension of an alternative and a low value on another dimension" (Payne, 1976, p. 367). When the number of options and the information regarding them multiply, thus adding to the complexity of the decision-making task, the individual is likely to switch from an optimizing strategy to a strategy that more quickly eliminates alternatives. Such an approach might involve a procedure in which the only alternatives retained are those that exceed a minimum level of acceptability on one important dimension. The decision maker might then switch back to an optimizing process once most options are eliminated.

Several researchers have applied these contingency models to career decisions. For instance, Gati (1986) suggested that individuals handle an array of occupational alternatives by sequentially evaluating the components of each alternative. Components are chosen for review depending on their importance to the individual. This is consistent with another model that suggests that a "good" career choice is one which is consistent with the individual's values (Krumboltz, Scherba, Hamel, & Mitchell, 1982). (See Slaney, 1988, for a review of cognitive models of career decisions.) Further research will be necessary to determine in what situations and under what conditions different decision strategies are used.

COMMITMENT PROCESS

How we make career decisions is tied to how we commit ourselves to those decisions and how our commitments influence the decisions we face. Commitment to a decision occurs when the decision is made under conditions of voluntary choice, when the decision is irrevocable, when the decision is made public, and when it is explicit and can be shown to have occurred (Salancik & Pfeffer, 1978). If an individual makes a selection from among several job possibilities, and if the selection becomes a matter of record, the individual is likely to develop a sense of commitment to the choice. As an example, an employee might be asked to choose a new project assignment from among a number of alternatives. It would then be instrumental for the employee to make a public, perhaps written, certification of the choice. Once the selection is made, announced, and initiated, the individual will be more committed than if the project had simply been arbitrarily assigned.

"When individuals are committed to a situation, they tend to develop attitudes consistent with their committing behavior" (Salancik & Pfeffer, 1978, p. 231). Commitment involves retrospective rationalizing. Once people voluntarily choose to do something, they tend to interpret the decision positively, providing their own intrinsic justification for it.

Extrinsic reinforcers, such as pay raises or promotions, probably supply employees with further justification for having made a particular career decision. Yet it may also be true that organizations risk reduction of individual commitment when they impose career decisions or when they supply employees with justifications external to their own choice process. "Any characteristic of a person's choices or situation that reduces felt responsibility will also reduce commitment and satisfaction" (O'Reilly & Caldwell, 1981, p. 599).

There seems to be an *escalating cycle of commitment* for careers within organizations. The longer an individual's organizational tenure, the more probable it is that the individual will feel committed to the organization (Buchanan, 1974). However, an individual's propensity to commitment building seems to vary with the stage of organizational tenure (Hall & Nougaim, 1968). For instance, during the career advancement stage (Years 2–4), individuals tend to seek job experiences that allow them to contribute significantly to the workings of the organization. If these people are handed assignments that enable them to make important contributions, and if the value of their contributions is recognized by the organization, then they are more likely to act and feel committed. Thus, organizations can increase commitment to the job and the organization, presumably affecting reactions to future career opportunities.

In summary, how committed we are to our jobs and to the organization is likely to influence the decisions we make. In addition, how we make decisions influences our commitment to the choice. The next section extends the discussion of the role of the organization in affecting decision and commitment processes and the value we place on different career opportunities.

ORGANIZATIONAL INFLUENCES ON CAREER DECISION MAKING

This section considers organizational factors that influence the career decisions people make, the decision processes they use, and what factors are important to them when evaluating alternatives. Space does not permit an in-depth treatment of each of these factors. Here we review them briefly to understand the complex environment in which career decisions take place.

We begin this section with a discussion of how organizations influence employees' commitment to their career decisions. Then we cover other ways organizations impact career decisions, specifically, opportunities for promotion, the willingness of the organization to address individuals' nonwork needs and values, and the openness of the organization to hiring and advancing women and minorities. Additional organizational characteristics we examine are the organization's structure and degree of formalization, organizational uncertainty and conflicting interests, the amount of movement of people in the organization, organizational values, and information and social processes.

Increasing Commitment

As indicated earlier, commitment can be fostered by the organization's approach to its employees. Organizations affect commitment by the types of opportunities they offer, and also by the freedom they give to individuals to take advantage of available opportunities.

When the organization provides more important task assignments to those in the advancement stage, it may wish to furnish first-year (establishment stage) employees with information about what to expect (Stumpf & Rabinowitz, 1981). This will create more realistic expectations. It also will tend to increase the possibility that the individual will remain with the organization rather than resign in response to frustrated expectations.

Opportunities for Promotion

Mobley (1982) presented a model for employee turnover in which the expected desirability of future work roles within the organization encourages employees to stay on, even if they are not satisfied with their present jobs. Thus, anticipation of later satisfaction may influence current career decision making. This effect is compounded when information from the organization directs the employee's attention to the probability of future opportunities. If the employee perceives those opportunities as being relevant to his or her values, the effect is again strengthened. This points to the utility of developing career management programs for individuals in organizations (London, 1983). As employees perceive the relevance of future opportunities within the organization, they will be more likely to decide to remain within the organization.

Nonwork Needs and Values

Earlier, we discussed the importance of the organization realizing that people at different career stages have different needs and face different career decisions. The willingness of the organization to address individual nonwork roles, and work and nonwork values, is a related issue. As our culture becomes more diverse, individuals are increasingly taking into account whether an organization is responsive to such issues as child care, dual-career couples, flexible work hours, slower tracking, and a variety of other personal considerations (Bailyn, 1980; Mobley, 1982). Organizations may or may not be responsive, but their posture will affect the decision making of employees within the organization as well as that of individuals considering entry.

Behavior Toward Minorities and Women

Headlining an article in *The Wall Street Journal* were the words, "Many Blacks Jump Off the Corporate Ladder to be Entrepreneurs: Feeling Their Rise Limited, They Launch ... Other Firms". An organization's attitudes toward its minority and female members has impact on whether these individuals are retained. Charles Grant, past president of the National Black M.B.A. Association, recently noted that as a Black in corporate management, "sooner or later you'll hit a bottleneck." "Then you've got to decide whether to keep banging on the door to go higher, or go it alone" (Hymowitz, 1984, p. 1). Whether an organization offers possibilities for advancement beyond a certain level is a special career decision issue for women and minorities. "Organizational initiatives designed to recruit, support, or improve the performance of women managers are not common" (London & Stumpf, 1982, p. 88). Openness to flexible work schedules is also rare, and it is especially important for women with children. The issue of sexual harassment in the workplace suggests a severely stressful situation requiring reactions that impact career decisions. (For a discussion of reactions to sexual harassment in the workplace, see Farley, 1978, and the U.S. Merit Systems Protection Board, 1981.)

Structure and Formalization

Organizations differ in their organizational structure and in the amount and kind of formalization they provide for their procedures (Stumpf & London, 1981). In highly structured organizations where employees can rely on a certain amount of regularity and consistency in approach, individuals are more able to predict when and on what basis promotions will be offered. Their career decision making can proceed in light of such knowledge.

Related to structure and formalization of procedures is the system by which the organization itself makes decisions, especially decisions regarding employee selection and advancement. Some organizations such as the military generate clearly stated decision processes for employee appraisal and resultant promotions (Morrison & Cook, 1983; Morrison, Martinez, & Townsend, 1984). Other organizations may be less methodical in their decision making, yet research shows that even "unstructured" decision processes manifest an underlying order that provides an element of predictability for employees once they are sufficiently socialized into the company to detect unwritten rules (Mintzberg, Raisinghani, & Theoret, 1976).

Uncertainty and Conflicting Interests

Continuing the discussion of how organizations make decisions about people, organizations may also call on more than one decision strategy, depending on the environmental conditions surrounding the problem. For instance, the level of *uncertainty* or *conflict of interest* in the organization will affect which decision strategy is most appropriate (Grandori, 1984). In the case of uncertainty, when the full range of alternatives and consequences for a particular problem are unknown, an *optimizing strategy*, which involves choosing the best alternative from among all relevant alternatives, would not be as suitable as a *satisficing strategy,* in which the search process ends as soon as the first acceptable option is encountered. For instance, if the choice situation were an unfilled job vacancy, an organization would have at least two available options (a) to mount an extensive search to gain information about all acceptable candidates before choosing one, or (b) to go with the first acceptable candidate to appear. If the organization did not have the time or the resources necessary for an optimizing process, a satisficing strategy might be the best approach.

In a case in which many conflicting interests are represented in the decision process, an *incremental strategy* might be preferable to an optimizing strategy. An incremental strategy requires making small decisional moves toward a larger decision, and so reduces risk. An optimizing strategy calls for a more integrative approach necessitating collective agreement, a state difficult to achieve when competing interests are involved (Grandori, 1984). As an example, a situation might arise in which a committee overseeing promotions reaches a deadlock on promoting a particular employee because some committee members are interested in advancing the person, whereas other members are not, and still others are more interested in promoting other employees. The best strategy might be incremental—to choose to give several individuals more challenging assignments in their current jobs. Such a decision might be preferable to risking advancement, yet would still achieve some of the benefits accompanying advancement, such as determining how well the individuals perform at a higher skill level. An optimizing strategy would call for gathering further, perhaps useless, data regarding the individuals and the promotion slot and then making the promotion decision. It would also require a consensus on the part of conflicting committee members.

Mobility

Organizational mobility, or the frequency and pattern of job movement within the organization, affects the opportunities open to employees and thus impacts their career decision making. Organizational characteristics conceptually related to internal job mobility are technology, structure, size, and unionization (Vardi, 1980). Organizational attributes such as the type of work roles available, the available channels for movement, and the criteria for movement are also important.

A problem many organizations face today is that mobility within the organization is restricted because of employee cutbacks, particularly in middle management, to reduce costs and be more competitive. Public organizations are experiencing the same pressures to cut costs and bureaucratic red tape. In the military, a problem affecting mobility is the importance of maintaining skills in specialty areas and subspecialties. This requires rotating officers between positions. But this is costly and logistically difficult when there is little or no organizational growth.

Organizational Values

An organization's values can influence the individual's decision making in a number of ways. Beliefs that possess widespread currency in the organization inform the individual as to what expectations, attitudes, needs, and reasons for action are acceptable, thus shaping the employee's thinking and behavior (O'Reilly & Caldwell, 1981; Salancik & Pfeffer, 1978).

In line with this discussion concerning the restricted opportunities for mobility that many organizations are experiencing, values are changing about the importance of movement. Rather than emphasizing job security as an important value, organizations are telling employees that career changes are acceptable in light of organizational constraints. Some organizations even help their employees find positions elsewhere. In addition, organizations are de-emphasizing the importance of promotion. Opportunities for achievement, risk taking, and skill development are becoming primary values.

Information and Social Processes

Social information impacts the decision process by drawing employees' attention to selected aspects of the environment. When co-workers or representatives of the organization point out the value of a given behavior, when issues are repeatedly discussed, or when the same interpretation of an action is shared by many employees, these pieces of information become salient to employees. Employees then use the information as cues for determining what is most important in the context of the organization (Salancik & Pfeffer, 1978). For instance, some corporations make career information and guidance available to their employees on a regular and visible basis. It is likely that employees in these organizations will come to share the view that career planning is important to them personally. If they believe they need career planning, the next logical step is for them to engage in it.

ENVIRONMENTAL CONDITIONS INFLUENCING CAREER DECISIONS

We use the term *environment* here to refer to conditions outside the individual and the organization that influence career decisions. The environment includes conditions that influence the individual directly, such as family responsibilities. The environment also includes social and economic conditions that impact organizations.

The external environment exerts an indirect but powerful influence on the type and number of career opportunities open to the employee in an organization.

> Opportunities within the organizations are influenced by the demand for labor, derived from the demand for products or services. Thus, the greater demand for organizational output, the greater the number of vacancies. That is, both the labor market and the nature of the firms's product markets influence the level of vacancies: the higher the rate of unemployment, the lower the number of opportunities in the firm. (Anderson, Milkovich, & Tsui, 1981, p. 532)

Another example might be governmental standards or judicial rulings that require organizations to make public their promotion criteria. Such regulations help avoid discrimination, but they also give employees a clearer notion of what to expect from the organization.

The presence of desirable job alternatives outside the organization also affects individual career decision making (Mobley, 1982). Perceptions of these alternatives may be as important as actual outside labor and market conditions. "Although economic conditions and the labor market may be unfavorable, one's unique skills, experience, and network of friends and acquaintances may create high expectations for career exploration success" (Stumpf, Colarelli, & Hartman, 1983, p. 195). If individuals believe there are opportunities external to the organization and if they expect to attain career goals, then the likelihood of their pursuing these alternatives is higher even though turnover is always somewhat dependent on actual environmental conditions (Mobley, 1982; Stumpf et al., 1983).

INDIVIDUAL CHARACTERISTICS AFFECTING CAREER DECISIONS

Next we turn to how individual characteristics influence career decision making. We discuss commitment to the choice of the job and organization from a developmental viewpoint, integrating what we have already covered about the influence of career stages and organizational conditions. Then we consider other individual characteristics including cognitive style, career motivation, career strategies, gender and minority status, nonwork responsibilities and interests, and values. These individual factors are affected by and interact with organizational and environmental conditions to affect career decisions.

Commitment and Career Stage

As stated earlier, there is a developmental aspect to the progression of individuals' careers within organizations. Employees' commitment to the organization increases with the number of years they have served the organization (Buchanan, 1974). The more years they have spent in the organization, the more likely they are to stay in it. At different tenure stages within the organization, different variables have a stronger impact on the level of commitment to the organization. For instance, during Years 2–4 with an organization, the employee typically experiences uncertainty as to the suitability of his or her career choice.

Decision Style

Decision style is the approach you generally use when you make a decision. Some people find it difficult to vary their decision style to meet the situation. In fact, many people have favorite styles or strategies they rely on perhaps because the strategies worked in the past. According to one view there are three types of decision styles: rational, intuitive, and dependent (Harren, 1979; Phillips, Friedlander, & Kost, 1985). A person's approach to decision making may be characterized by one predominant style, elements of all three styles, or a variety of styles changing from one decision to the next. Each style is described here.

Rational Style.   This involves systematic appraisal and logical delibera-
tion with an expanded time perspective.   Rational decision makers accept
responsibility for decision making, anticipate the consequences of previous
and current decisions, and gather and weigh information carefully, thor-
oughly, and objectively.

Intuitive Style.   Intuitive decision makers tend to be emotional and impul-
sive.   These individuals accept responsibility for the decision, as do rational
decision makers.   However, the intuitive style relies heavily on fantasy,
attention to present feelings, and emotional self-awareness.

Dependence Style.   People who use a dependent style assign responsibility for choice to external events or to other people.   These individuals are
passive, compliant, and heavily influenced by other's expectations.   They
have a difficult time making important decisions by themselves, and generally
need a lot of encouragement and support in making decisions.

Positive and Negative Problem Solving.   Some people have a *positive*
approach to problem solving.   People who evaluate their problem solving
capabilities positively say they have self-confidence and personal control
when solving problems.   These individuals are generally more confident
about their decision-making ability and potential for career success.   They are
more likely to choose an occupational field related to their abilities, and they
are less likely to blame others or circumstances for their indecision.   Those
with a *negative* self-appraisal of their problem solving lack self-confidence,
avoid problems, and express little personal control.   This is not to say they
cannot make a decision.   Rather, it is likely that negative problem solvers
make poor career decisions.

Career Motivation and Maturity

Related to cognitive style is the individual's *career motivation.* London (1983,
1985) conceptualized career motivation as "a multidimensional construct
internal to the individual, influenced by the situation, and reflected in the
individual's decisions and behaviors" (London, 1983, p. 620). The dimensions
of individual career motivation are career identity, career insight, and career
resilience. One's career identity reflects the importance of a career to one's
sense of self. Career insight is the realism of the individual's view of self, the
organization, and career goals. Career resilience includes self-confidence,
the desire for achievement, a willingness to take risks, and the ability to act
independently and cooperatively as appropriate to the situation.   These

concepts, although developed independently, are analogous to the concepts of vocational identity, the need for information and reassurance, and the need to face barriers. These concepts have been applied to career decision situations by Holland, Daiger, and Power (1980).

A related concept is career maturity. Individuals who are high in career maturity make career decisions in a way that can be characterized as involved, decisive, independent, task-oriented (e.g., understanding what work is like), and willing to compromise between needs and reality (Betz, 1988; Crites, 1978).

Career Strategies

Career strategies include: (a) creating career opportunities, (b) becoming more involved in work, (c) presenting oneself in a positive light, (d) seeking career guidance, (e) networking, (f) adopting others' opinions, and (g) other enhancement (e.g., demonstrating respect for top managers but not ingratiating yourself to them) (Gould & Penley, 1984). These strategies are hypothesized to speed the rate of upward mobility. Other enhancement, creating opportunities, extending work involvement, and opinion conformity positively correlate with rate of salary progression.

Nonwork Responsibilities and Interests

Nonwork variables influence individual career decision making (London & Stumpf, 1982; Tinsley & Tinsley, 1988). Nonwork values and nonwork roles are related to employee turnover (Mobley, 1982). Nonwork roles include marital status, family membership, parenthood, leisure interests, religious and altruistic commitments, and being part of a dual-career couple. Nonwork values are linked to nonwork roles. They reflect beliefs and preferences in regard to lifestyle, geographic location, religious and cultural affiliations, family orientation, and social practices. The individual who wishes to remain close to his or her family or hometown, or whose spouse and children prefer not to move, is probably less likely to accept a promotion to a new location than the employee who is unmarried and childless, and eager for novel experiences.

Values

Alongside nonwork roles and values stand the individual's *work values*. Although some individuals possess career motivation in high degree from early on in their work life, others follow "the slow-burn way to the top" (Bailyn, 1980). There are those who refuse promotions or who, at mid-life, decide to take a less prestigious job. These people choose an alternative route to the traditional career path, perhaps because they lack talent or motivation. Some people simply prefer reduced pressure, and others prefer job challenge to advancement. Bailyn's research shows that "slow-burners" often anticipate a rising career trajectory, yet they seem to prefer more flexibility and less intensity in the workplace and so choose a slower pace.

Sex and Minority Group Status

Sex and minority group membership are two other factors affecting the outcome of individuals' career decisions. Women with two or more children are less likely to be fully involved in their careers than either men or than women with one or no children (Bailyn, 1980). Social class may be a more important determinant of occupational aspiration and attainment than is race, with people from higher classes being most likely to achieve socially valued positions (Osipow, 1983). With an 83% rise in Blacks classified as managers from 1972 to 1982, a more positive relationship between race and vocational achievement is expected to develop. Despite this, as we stated earlier, a recent trend is for Black managers to leave corporations in favor of starting their own businesses (Hymowitz, 1984). They reportedly feel that movement up the corporate ladder will be limited by their race.

Individual-Situation Interaction

The aforementioned points to the interactional effect produced by the interplay between the individual and his or her environment. Individual behavior cannot be understood apart from the context in which it occurs. Thus, the context is an important source of information regarding individual behavior. Yet, as with people adjusting to a new work role by transforming the role itself, individuals can to some extent alter their surroundings (Nicholson, 1984). Career mobility "is a function of the *interaction* between organizational attributes (which establish the type of roles, the available channels, and the criteria for career movement) and individual level determinants (demographic characteristics as well as behavioral processes)" (Vardi, 1980, p. 347).

PRACTICAL IMPLICATIONS

Given our review of the nature and process of career decision making the question becomes how can we use this to influence career decisions for the good of the individual and the organization? Of primary importance is the realization that an organization's policies, structures, values, and handling of information can influence individual decision making.

The organization's attitudes toward its workers are also important. Are employees seen as valuable resources to be carefully developed? Does the organization give support to individual career decision making and planning? Is attention paid to the variation of individual needs at different career stages?

For instance, the employee's socialization into the company during the first year of employment is an especially promising time for encouraging organization commitment. Newcomers bring with them a variety of expectations regarding their jobs. There is often a discrepancy between these expectations and reality (Louis, 1980a,1980b). If the organization prepares the individual by providing a realistic preview of the job and if the individual is helped to see attractive future prospects within the organization, then chances of retaining the recruit are heightened.

Stimulating good career decision making on the part of employees contributes to the overall vitality of an organization. People who have adequately assessed both themselves and the environment before making a career decision are more likely to be satisfied with their choice and more committed to the organization if they decide to remain within it (Greenhaus & Sklarew, 1981; Stumpf et al., 1983). Encouraging career planning and providing realistic information, especially early in the employee's career, will highlight the value of the employee to the organization and, as mentioned, may also help close the gap between expectations and reality.

Methods of Influencing Career Decisions

There are a number of methods by which career decisions may be influenced for the good of both the individual and the organization. Examples of these methods are described here under three headings: organizational policies and programs, supervision processes, and vehicles for individual initiatives.

Organizational Policies and Programs. These include actions inaugurated by the organization itself. Some of these actions are listed here.

1. *Information* regarding career opportunities may be made available to employees, increasing their knowledge of opportunities available within the organization and demonstrating the relevance of these opportunities to their lives. Such information can enhance employee recruitment as well as retention.

2. *Career paths* can be tailor-made for employees. When individuals are

involved in mapping out their own careers, they have the opportunity to choose from among a number of alternatives. This tends to make them more satisfied with their eventual decisions and thus more likely to commit themselves to the decisions. Offering individuals a choice from a number of standard career paths and training opportunities is one way of encouraging this.

3. *Planning Mechanisms* such as formalized career planning worksheets or career path proposals may encourage employees to institute planning and decision making for their careers.

4. *Programs for orientation and acclimation* can be presented to new employees. These programs enhance individuals' knowledge of the organization, increase the reality of expectations, and motivate them to begin immediately on career planning.

5. *Training and development programs* are regularly offered by many organizations. Special career development for new managers, high potential employees, and standard career track managers are typical options (see London, 1985, for examples of these programs).

6. *Positive reinforcement* can be awarded in the form of verbal praise, assignment of desirable projects, salary increases, promotions, and other incentives for good performance. Such rewards tend to encourage desirable work behavior and to strengthen job satisfaction.

7. *Opportunities for achievement* may be advanced to employees to provide them with a sense of accomplishment, with recognition, and with occasions for contributing something of more than passing value to the organization. When individuals feel their work is important to the organization, they tend to be more satisfied and may decide to exert extra energy to their work roles. The likelihood of retention is optimized when employees understand the value of their contributions.

Supervision Processes.   The employee's immediate supervisor is in a position to have a significant impact on individual career progression. Simply following good management practices can make the supervisor more helpful. Some organizations encourage bosses of new managers to initiate career planning with their subordinates. Bosses do not always know how to go about such planning, nor are they rewarded for doing so. Following are several suggestions that should enhance supervisors' oversight of their employees' career planning and decision making.

1. *Boss training* enables bosses to know and effectively make use of the determinants affecting individual career motivation, career planning, and decision making. As stated earlier, career resilience, career insight, and

career identity are three domains of individual career motivation (London, 1983). These domains affect how the individual goes about making career decisions. Supervisors who can guide employees' choices in light of their career motivation will probably be more effective.

2. *Rewarding bosses for developing their subordinates* increases the likelihood that the organization will have a positive impact on its workers' career decisions. When bosses' job responsibilities include career development with and for subordinates, and when bosses are reinforced in some way for carrying this responsibility out, more bosses will probably engage in employee career planning.

3. *Job and work group design* involves supervisors modifying job characteristics to suit the individual needs of employees. Amount of job autonomy, level of accountability, opportunities for achievement and creativity, and the nature of nonwork roles and values are variants to be considered in designing jobs and work groups tailor-made for the individuals involved. Bosses need to know what they can do in working with subordinates to enhance their job challenge through job redesign.

Vehicles for Individual Initiatives. Organizations may offer opportunities for assistance with the process, and supervisors may provide oversight, but career planning and decision making is ultimately in the hands of the individual employee. Brief and Aldag (1981) acknowledged this when they recommended a more "proactive" role for individuals in organizations. Such a role requires a certain amount of initiative to take advantage of opportunities for career development provided within the company. More enterprising employees often go beyond regular offerings inside and outside the company. Some common methods for individually initiated actions are listed here.

1. *Training,* such as courses, special workshops, and lectures may be provided by the organization, and are frequently made available by outside groups as well. Some organizations provide tuition aid for those who wish to take advantage of outside training. Supervisors may recommend specific educational experiences to their subordinates. Workshops may provide help in career planning and decision making by disseminating career information or by providing instruction on decision-making skills or goal setting.

2. *Self-assessment* methods of two types have had particular appeal. The first consists of self-assessment procedures provided by the company. Generally, they involve going through a sequence of instructor-led workbooks or through workshops that help people analyze their skills and motivation. Career planning is often the outcome of such procedures.

The other approach, self-administered self-assessment guides, can be found in many books and manuals even in the form of computer software. As an example, the American College Testing Program has designed a computer program called "Discover." The five-module package is intended for microcomputers. Individuals administer it to themselves in attempting to plan their career development within an organization.

3. *Career motivation assessment* is an in-depth process that may take place in an assessment center over a number of days (London, 1985). Career motivation assessment provides information regarding the individual's career motivation. Other factors may also be measured. These include personality variables, mode of interpersonal relationships, cognitive style, self-perception, and sensitivity to social, especially organizational, environments. Career motivation assessment can be especially helpful to those who have no clear sense of career direction.

4. *Motivation awareness training* is geared to employees with a more developed degree of self-awareness. Motivation awareness training assists individuals in learning the characteristics of career motivation and planning, and how these characteristics apply to themselves. Such a process may be more or less personalized, depending on training designs and the intent of trainers.

5. *Development journals or diaries* exist to help individuals keep track of their job-related experiences and to monitor them over time. This gives a clearer sense of the direction a career has taken. Thus, employees can discern whether they wish to move in other directions. Then they can determine what forms of self-development might be needed. Of course, keeping a diary is not necessary for self-reflection. Our point is that it is valuable for people to regularly think about the linkages between their strengths and weaknesses, their career goals, and the extent to which job events and experiences contribute to goal accomplishment.

AN EXAMPLE

We conclude this discussion with a brief example that demonstrates ways that one corporation provides support for employees' career decisions and development and ties its career programs to the strategic needs of the organization.

This firm, like many others, faced increased global competition and advancing technology. The human resources staff worked closely with line executives to develop a human performance system that would prepare and reward employees for increasing their responsiveness to customers and for continuously updating their skills to take advantage of changing technology.

The resulting career programs were strategically linked to helping the organization accomplish its goals and helping employees develop within the changing corporate context. Employees were presented with alternative career options, directions for development, and opportunities to broaden their skills and enhance their contribution to the firm.

Specifically, four career enhancement programs were designed:

1. a professional development program to increase employees' knowledge of the business, the competitive environment, and the importance of customer satisfaction and quality improvement;
2. a mastery path program for job families to ensure that employees learn the skills required on particular jobs;
3. a supervisor training program to help supervisors understand their role as developers and coaches of their subordinates; and
4. a career support system to provide employees with information about career opportunities and to provide a mechanism for annual career planning.

Professional Development.   The professional development program took the form of a series of modules, each introduced in a booklet. The booklet explained the purpose of the module, allowed employees to assess their own performance on the module, and asked employees to meet with their supervisors to agree on a development related to the topic of the module. The module topics were new technology, quality improvement, people management, and customer responsiveness. All employees were expected to complete the four modules during a 2-year period. The development plan for each individual varied depending on the individual s existing level of expertise and experience. The supervisor evaluated the employee's progress on each module as part of the annual performance appraisal.

Mastery Paths.   A "mastery path" was developed for each key job family (groups of similar jobs). A mastery path consisted of employee selection criteria, training curricula, job experiences, and methods for supervisory evaluation that led to job mastery. A mastery path was for new employees and existing employees who were still learning their position or who needed performance improvement. Developed by teams of employees who were experts on their jobs, a mastery path helped individuals understand what was expected of them to achieve a desired level of expertise and performance. It structured a developmental process and provided direction for supervisors to work with new employees. Supervisors determined when their subordinates achieved mastery, which took about 1 year for a given job. The employee then stayed in the same position for one or more additional years before being promoted or transferred to a new position that would put him or her on a new mastery path.

Supervisor Training.   A new course, entitled "The Supervisor as Coach and Developer," was implemented to help supervisors understand the importance of setting goals, giving performance feedback, offering advice, and providing information about the organization. Role play exercises helped participants practice goal setting, counseling, and feedback principles.

Career Information and Planning Support.   The human resources department established a career development function, and line departments established career resource centers and implemented career planning policies and procedures. Forms were designed for annual career planning and supervisory review of career plans. Information packets were prepared to communicate to employees where job opportunities would be during the next several years and what skills were required to take advantage or these opportunities. Tuition aid was established to support employees who were pursuing advanced degrees that were company-related (i.e., that the supervisor agreed would be valuable to the company in the employee's current job or in another position). A training curriculum of in-house managerial courses was established to support the professional development modules and mastery path requirements described earlier.

In addition, an "upward feedback" process was implemented that asked subordinates to anonymously rate their supervisors on dimensions of leadership and support for career development. Supervisors were provided with a report of their subordinates' average responses. This information was to be used by supervisors to help guide their development. (The upward feedback results were not used by higher management to evaluate the supervisor's performance in order to reduce any perceived threat from being evaluated by one's subordinates and increase acceptance of the program.)

All of these programs are updated annually to reflect business changes. For instance, the leadership dimensions included in the upward feedback process were changed as the performance expectations of the business changed—for instance, the dimension of "empowerment" was added when the firm increased focus on empowering subordinates to make their own decisions. As more work was done in quality improvement teams, training courses were designed to help employees improve their negotiation and conflict resolution skills.

When technological developments decreased the need for technical employees in operations departments, opportunities were provided for individuals to move into marketing to increase the firm's sales and improve customer support. Information about mastery paths in marketing positions was provided to give employees realistic job previews. Assessment processes were established to select employees who had the potential to be successful in a marketing position. Increased training was made available. Thus, employees were presented with opportunities within the firm for new career directions that met organizational needs. Support was provided to help the employee make the decision to apply, and then development was available to help the individual be successful.

Overall, this example demonstrates that multiple, integrated approaches are needed to support employees' career decision making and development. Moreover, these programs should be refined over time to reflect changing organizational needs. The programs provide the supporting elements outlined in Fig. 6.1. In addition, the programs provide the vehicles for individual initiative outlined in the figure (e.g., self-assessment, and training).

Despite the benefits of the programs in this example, more could be done by the firm to incorporate knowledge of individual decision-making processes (e.g., satisficing strategies) in helping employees to use information about career opportunities and helping supervisors to understand their subordinates' career stage, goals, and commitments. The programs could be refined further to recognize relevant individual characteristics including life stage, family needs and other nonwork concerns, and different values. Given the increased heterogeneity of the workforce and the need to manage employee diversity in many firms, the organization should appreciate that people differ in their career goals and the opportunities they desire. At the same time, employees need to understand the organization's changing goals and how their career ambitions can be met, or may need to be adjusted, to match the organization's changing needs.

SUMMARY

This chapter explored the individual and environmental factors influencing career choices, developed a framework for describing individual career decision making in the organizational context, and considered the implications of these for organizational policies and procedures regarding career development.

The premises of the chapter were that there are multiple factors affecting career decisions, that career choices involve changes within work roles as well as transitions from one work role to another, and that decision making may be initiated by the individual or by an opportunity offered to the individual. The rational processes accompanying career decision making are both prospective and retrospective.

The implications of the chapter include the belief that increased knowledge of the decision process should be used to influence career decision making for the good of the individual and the organization. The organization's policies, structure, and handling of information all affect employee decision making. The organization needs to be attentive to this as well as to be supportive of individuals' differing needs at differing career stages. This requires a proactive personnel department that designs appropriate programs and that is listened to when it alerts management individual needs and vehicles for organizational support.

Stimulating good decision making based on accurate and adequate information contributes to the vitality of an organization. Employees who have assessed both themselves and the environment before making a career decision are more likely to be satisfied with their choices. Encouraging career planning and providing realistic information early in an employee's career highlights the value of the employee to the organization, lessens the gap between employee expectations and reality, and increases the probability that individuals will choose a career path that is best for them and the organization.

REFERENCES

Anderson, J. C., Milkovich, G. T., & Tsui, A. (1981). A model of intraorganizational mobility. *Academy of Management Review, 6*(4), 529–538.

Bailyn, L. (1980). The slow burn way to the top: Some thoughts on the early years of organizational careers. In C. B. Derr (Ed.), *Work, family and the career: New frontiers in theory and research* (pp. 94–106). New York: Praeger.

Betz, N. E. (1988). The assessment of career development and maturity. In W. B. Walsh & S. H. Osipow (Eds.),*Career decision making* (pp. 77–136). Hillsdale, NJ: Lawrence Erlbaum Associates.

Brief, A. P., & Aldag, R. J. (1981). The "self" in work organizations: A conceptual review. *Academy of Management Review, 6*(1), 75–88.

Brown, D. (1970). *Students' vocational choices: A review and critique.* Boston: Houghton Mifflin.

Brown, D., Brooks, L., & Associates. (1984). *Career choice and development.* San Francisco: Jossey-Bass.

Buchanan, B. (1974). Building organizational commitment: The socialization of manager in work organizations. *Administrative Science Quarterly, 19,* 533–546.

Crites, J. O. (1978). *Career maturity inventory: Theory and research handbook* (2nd ed.). New York: McGraw-Hill.

Farley, L. (1978). *Sexual shakedown: The sexual harassment of women on the job.* New York: McGraw-Hill.

Gati, I. (1986). Making career decisions: A conceptual frame of reference for counseling. *Journal of Counseling Psychology, 33,* 408–417.

Gould, S., & Penley, L. E. (1984). Career strategies and salary progression: A study of their relationships in a municipal bureaucracy. *Organizational Behavior and Human Performance, 34,* 244–265.

Grandori, A. (1984). A prescriptive contingency view of organizational decision making. *Administrative Science Quarterly, 29,* 192–209.

Greenhaus, J. H., & Sklarew, N. D. (1981). Some sources and consequences of career exploration. *Journal of Vocational Behavior, 18,* 1–12.

Hall, D. T. (1976). *Careers in organizations.* Santa Monica, CA: Goodyear.

Hall, D. T., & Nougaim, K. E. (1968). An examination of Maslow's need hierarchy in an organizational setting. *Organizational Behavior and Human Performance, 3,* 12–35.

Harren, B. A. (1979). A model of career decision making for college students. *Journal of Vocational Behavior, 14,* 119–130.

Holland, J. L., Daiger, D. C., & Power, P. G. (1980). *My vocational situation.* Palo Alto, CA: Consulting Psychologists Press.

Hymowitz, C. (1984, August). Many blacks jump off the corporate ladder to be entrepreneurs. *The Wall Street Journal,* pp. 1, 16.

Krumboltz, J. D., Scherba, D. S., Hamel, D. A., & Mitchell, L. K. (1982). Effect of training in rational decision making on the quality of simulated career decisions. *Journal of Counseling Psychology, 29,* 619–625.

Levinson, D. J. (1977). The mid-life transition: A period in adult psychosocial development. *Psychiatry, 40,* 99–112.

London, M. (1983). Toward a theory of career motivation. *Academy of Management Review, 8*(4), 620–630.

London, M. (1985). *Developing managers.* San Francisco: Jossey-Bass.

London, M., & Stumpf, S. (1982). *Managing careers.* Reading, MA: Addison-Wesley.

Louis, M. R. (1980a). Career transitions: Varieties and commonalities. *Academy of Management Review, 5*(3), 329–340.

Louis, M. R. (1980b). Surprise and sense making: What newcomers experience in entering unfamiliar organizational settings. *Administrative Science Quarterly, 25,* 226–251.

Mihal, W. M., Sorce, P. A., & Comte, T. E. (1984). A process model of individual career decision making. *Academy of Management Review, 9*(1), 95–103.

Mintzberg, H., Raisinghani, D., & Theoret, A. (1976). The structure of "unstructured" decision processes. *Administrative Science Quarterly, 21,* 246–275.

Mobley, W. H. (1982). *Employee turnover: Causes and consequences.* Reading, MA: Addison-Wesley.

Morrison, R. F., & Cook, T. M. (1983, August). *Military officer career development and decision making: A multiple-cohort longitudinal analysis of the first twenty-four years.* Paper presented at the meeting of the American Psychological Association, Anaheim, CA.

Morrison, R. F., Martinez, C., & Townsend, F. W. (1984). *Officer career development: Description of aviation assignment decisions in the antisubmarine warfare (ASW) patrol community* (Report No. NPRDC TR 84-31). San Diego, CA: Navy Personnel Research and Development Center.

Neugarten, B. L. (1976). Adaptation and the life cycle. *The Counseling Psychologist, 6*(1), 16–20.

Nicholson, N. (1984). A theory of work role transitions. *Administrative Science Quarterly, 29,* 172–191.

O'Reilly, C. A., & Caldwell, D. F. (1981). The commitment and job tenure of new employees: Some evidence of postdecisional justification. *Administrative Science Quarterly, 26,* 597–616.

Osipow, S. H. (1983). *Theories of career development* (3rd ed.). Englewood Cliffs, NJ: Prentice-Hall.

Payne, J. W. (1976). Task complexity and contingent processing in decision making: An information search and protocol analysis. *Organizational Behavior and Human Performance, 16,* 366–387.

Phillips, S. D., Friedlander, M. L., Pazienza, N. J., & Kost, P. P. (1985). A factor analytic investigation of decision styles. *Journal of Vocational Behavior, 26,* 106–115.

Phillips, S. D., & Pazienza, N. J. (1988). History and theory of the assessment of career development and decision making. In W. B. Walsh & S. H. Osipow (Eds.), *Career decision making* (pp. 1–31). Hillsdale, NJ: Lawrence Erlbaum Associates.

Roberts, K. (1968). The entry into employment: An approach towards a general theory. *Sociological Review, 16,* 165–184.

Rothstein, W. G. (1980). The significance of occupations in work careers: An empirical and theoretical review. *Journal of Vocational Behavior, 17,* 328–343.

Salancik, G. R., & Pfeffer, J. (1978). A social information processing approach to job attitudes and task design. *Administrative Science Quarterly, 23,* 224–251.

Simon, H. A. (1976). *Administrative behavior* (3rd ed.). New York: The Free Press.

Slaney R. B. (1988). The assessment of career decision making. In W. B. Walsh & S. H. Osipow (Eds.), *Career decision making* (pp. 33–76). Hillsdale, NJ: Lawrence Erlbaum Associates.

Stumpf, S. A., Colarelli, S. M., & Hartman, K. (1983). Development of to career exploration survey (CES). *Journal of Vocational Behavior, 22,* 191–226.

Stumpf, S. A., & London, M. (1981). Management promotions: Individual and organizational factors influencing the decision process. *Academy of Management Review, 6*(4), 539–549.

Stumpf, S. A., & Rabinowitz, S. (1981). Career stage as a moderator of performance relationships with facets of job satisfaction and role perceptions. *Journal of Vocational Behavior, 18,* 202–218.

Super, D. E. (1957). *The psychology of careers.* New York: Harper & Row.

Tinsley, H. E. A., & Tinsley, D. J. (1988). An expanded context for the study of career decision making, development, and maturity. In W. B. Walsh & S. H. Osipow (Eds.), *Career decision making* (pp. 213–264). Hillsdale, NJ: Lawrence Erlbaum Associates.

Vardi, Y. (1980). Organizational career mobility: An integrative model. *Academy of Management Review, 5*(3), 341–355.

U. S. Merit Systems Protection Board. (1981). *Sexual harassment in the federal workplace, Is it a problem?* Washington, DC: Office of Merit Systems Review and Studies.

7

Twenty Questions: Research Needed to Advance the Field of Careers

Douglas T. Hall
Boston University

The preceding chapters in this book are testimony to both how far the field of career development has come since the 1960s and to how far we still have to go. Or, perhaps more precisely, it indicates the directions in which we have to go.

One of the exciting features of this book is that it has been provided by both practitioners and scholars in the area of careers. And much of the work represented here was heavily influenced by a period of intensive cross-fertilization of ideas during the Tri-Service Career Research Workshop (University of San Diego, 1984). Thus, not only are theory, research, and practice represented in these pages, but all three have had the opportunity to influence one another. Because career development is an applied field, it requires the interplay of theory and practice if it is to grow.

This chapter reflects on the topics and ideas from the workshop that have represented the main body of this book and raises some ideas about critical questions around which the field might advance.

This is not intended to be an exhaustive review of the career literature; that can be found in Greenhaus and Parasuraman (1986) and in Brown, Brooks, and Associates (1990). In addition, extensive reviews of specific topics in careers, as well as fresh ideas for future directions and new theory can be found in the *Handbook of Career Theory* (Arthur, Hall, & Lawrence, 1989b).

When I was growing up, a favorite game of mine was called "Twenty Questions," referring to the number of questions you were given to identify an unknown object (remember, animal, mineral, or vegetable?). This seems an appropriate format to help us figure out just what a career is all about, as well. Thus, this chapter centers around 20 questions that might be useful in advancing the state of theory, practice, and research.

THE 20 QUESTIONS

Mobility: Growth or Crisis?

As the Dewhirst and the Minor, Slade, and Meyers chapters (chapters 4 and 5, respectively) show, mobility represents probably one of the most interesting theoretical issues in the careers area, as well as one of the most critical practical concerns. It is also intriguing because it touches on so many different facets of the career: individual socialization, role innovation, stress, organizational career policies, career paths, meanings of success, personal versus organizational control over the career, career versus family conflict, and so on. Both of these chapters show clearly the link between a flexible workforce and a more adaptable, responsive organization. The model of the career transition process presented by Minor, Slade, and Meyer (in Fig. 5.1), based on the work of Louis, Brett, Nicholson and others, provides a practical guide to organizational career managers. The nice feature of a job-change transition is that it is limited in time, is easy to influence, and yet is a critical period for learning for the individual. The newly assigned person has a clear "need to know" in relation to the new position, so that any training, orientation, career planning, or other supportive activities will have strong impact.

Let us consider a few of the more critical questions related to career mobility that arose at the workshop.

Mobility and Performance.   Generally a personnel transfer is made to achieve some particular objective, usually an organizational one. However, there has been little research on the actual effects of a job move on performance. The work by Katz (1978), reviewed in the Minor, Slade, and Myers chapter, documents phases in the employee's adaptation to a new role (i.e., changing correlates of job attitudes over time), but it does not look specifically at performance. Such research should also take into account the purpose of the move. If it is primarily a developmental move, there may be a dip in performance while the person acquires the skills he or she was sent there to develop. If the move is cross-functional, for example, how long would it take for the person to get "up to speed"? Another factor might be the degree of fit or stretch between the skill profile of the old job and that of the new one. What is badly needed in many organizations with a history of within-function development, where there is a desire to encourage more cross-functional movement, is an indication of which pairs of functions are dissimilar enough to provide stretch and growth yet similar enough so that the person is not totally de-skilled by the move. We might call these *cousin functions*, because they are related, yet they demand different skills.

An example here would be a high-tech company that is considering moving engineers (traditionally the backbone of the company, who rarely move out of engineering) into production management assignments. There is enough technical engineering content in production (in fact, this is growing, with computer-aided manufacturing) to provide a good application of the engineer's skills (in fact, the engineer would probably help upgrade the technical sophistication of the production process). However, the plant job would contain enough new skill demands (e.g., supervisory skills, employee relations, planning, budgeting) that the move would require tremendous learning for the engineer. A method for measuring the amount of skill and psychological distance existing for various kinds of job moves has been proposed by Hall (1981). It is possible to construct a quantitative scale to measure the magnitude of change associated with a move, as a function of factors such as whether it is a new function, a new organization, a new geographic location, a new level, and so forth, or some combination of these factors. Thus, we might examine the following questions:

1. For a given job move (requiring a given amount of skill and psychological change), how does performance change over time, before and after the move? (This research would best be done for a type of job move that is made very frequently and that has important consequences for both individual development and organizational effectiveness, as the results would tend to be situation-specific.)

2. What is the acceptable trade-off between short-term performance and long-term skill development in a job move? How much of a short-term performance decrement is possible without having harmful effects on individual self-esteem and/or organizational functioning? Phrased another way, what is the optimal "stretch" in a job change?

3. Using a quantitative measure of change associated with a job move (Hall, 1981), what type(s) of moves would produce this optimal stretch?

4. Within a particular type of organization, industry, or profession, what are the most promising cousin functions for facilitating cross-functional mobility? The Dewhirst chapter provides good material for addressing this question.

Mobility and Well-Being. As discussed frequently at the workshop, we know more at this point about the effects of mobility on well-being than we know about mobility and performance. Before Brett's (1982) study, the major issue here was whether job moves have an adverse effect on the well-being of employees and their families. The intuitive response for many people might have been, "yes." We know now from Brett's study that mobility does not necessarily have harmful effects; in fact, a mobile lifestyle seems to have some positive effects on life satisfaction (but negative effects on social relationships). An extremely valuable integration and reconceptualization of recent work is found in Nicholson and West (1989).

At this point we need more research on the conditions that affect positive and negative reactions to job moves. Minor, Slade, and Myers propose some in their chapter: compatibility of transfer with employee's career development plans, clear definition and explanation of new job and its role in the person's future career development, early family involvement in planning the move, and information about financial implications of the move. These all describe company actions that would facilitate the move.

I would add another important company action: Someone in a position of responsibility should address seriously the question, "Is this move really necessary?" Too often companies have moves that have become traditional steps in a developmental sequence. Many traditional job moves have been rendered unnecessary (or even dysfunctional) in today's radically altered business environment. For example, new MBAs are often rotated through several corporate staff functions to help them find their niche. In fact, they may already have identified their chosen field as part of their MBA training. What might be more useful would be a field assignment in an operating role (e.g., an hourly job in a manufacturing facility or a sales position.) The work of McCall, Lombardo, and Morrison (1988) at the Center for Creative Leadership provides an important first step at categorizing types of developmental moves and the learnings they produce.

I would also propose some employee career and family characteristics that may also be related to the type of effect a move will have: career stage (easier in early career and perhaps midcareer); ages of children (easiest with no children or children under, say, 10; hardest with high school children); career status of spouse (harder with a career spouse); and plateaued versus nonplateaued status (less acceptable if plateaued). Thus, the following questions might be studied:

5. What organizational actions are most effective in moderating the effects of a job move so that it is a positive experience?

6. More generally, what is the overall impact on particular human resource policies that relate to mobility? For example, what effect does a promotion from within policy have? What are the effects of a policy of growing people within functions? What are the effects of a policy of cross-functional or cross-business movement? Are there certain levels at which cross-functional moves are unlikely to be successful? The foundation of such work could be Ford and Bhagat's model (chapter 3, this volume) of the alignment of reward systems in relation to the environment, time orientation,

current human resource practices, and resource allocation. In this case the critical environmental issue would be changing societal needs and expectations regarding the balance between work and family. Their approach would be a promising way to create fundamental cultural change in the organization around work/family relationships (Hall, 1990).

7. What personal, family, and career characteristics are related to positive experiences in a job move? Can we construct a profile of a type of employee and family who would be especially at risk in a move?

8. Is there an interaction between type of employee, company action, and type of move (as discussed earlier in Questions 1–4)? What types of moves work best for which groups of employees or for what types of companies? The military now moves senior people much more than junior people. Industry, in some fields, does the opposite. Which approach is more effective?

(One way to categorize companies for this type of research would be in terms of their human resource movement policies, as discussed in Question 6).

Career and Family

We have just discussed family issues as they affect and are in turn affected by job moves. It is worth adding, however, that the relationship between work and family has become a critical component of the careers literature. For a detailed discussion of the sources of conflict between these two domains, see Greenhaus and Beutell (1985) and Voyandoff (1988). Greenhaus and Beutell's article contains many straightforward and easily testable propositions about the connections between home and work.

It seems to me that we need to get beyond the issue of whether and how much work and family affect each other. The next step is to focus on the processes by which the two areas interact. By process, I do not mean the old issues of whether the two have compensatory or spillover effects, but rather in what specific ways does work intrude on family life, just why does work involvement manage to drive out personal time so often (and why does the opposite not occur), and so forth.

A promising method in this area has been proposed by Judith Richter (1983). This method looks at daily transitions between home and work as a process of crossing the boundaries of the two domains. By detailed studies of boundary characteristics and boundary passages, the characteristics of the two domains and of their interface become much clearer. A more recent version of this work is found in Hall and Richter (1988).

These issues, then, in the work–family area can be stated as follows:

9. What are the specific forms of strain between career and home life? How do these vary as a function of career characteristics, interpersonal

support, and organizational characteristics? (See Hall, 1990, for recommendations on organizational changes to accommodate work–family issues).

10. In what specific ways do the boundaries of the work and home domains operate? What are the types of transitions people make across these boundaries? How do these transitions vary with gender, type of work, organizational characteristics, family, and career stage?

Diversity in Mobility Rates and Company Growth

Now that there is such diversity in growth rates of companies, as Dewhirst suggests in chapter 4, we need to go beyond the descriptive earlier work of Veiga (1981) and examine the correlates of different mobility rates as a function of the life cycle or growth rate of the organization. We would probably find that even in growing organizations in 1990, mobile managers may be moving at a rate closer to that of the plateaued managers when Veiga collected his data.

In fact, in this era of corporate downsizing and restructuring, we do not hear as much about the problems of plateauing as we did in the 1980s. The issue seems to have been reframed as one of the need for promoting adaptability and career redirection. In a sense, we have moved beyond plateauing. (Indeed, in most organizations, those who are "only" plateaued are the fortunate ones! However, plateauing is at best a warning signal for the individual to initiate some serious career planning.)

The organization's growth rate may moderate the impact of mobility on development and well-being. If the company is stagnating, this may increase the need for mobility (or at least a within-location job change), because the stimulation of change is less likely to come from the job. Ironically, then, organizational financial difficulties may force the firm to engage in some of the work assignment changes that Dewhirst calls for (in his Table 4.5) to combat plateauing. In a similar vein, a person who has not moved in 5 years in a rapidly growing firm may really be dead-ended.

How is the slow-growth or declining organization dealing with high-potential employees and with related processes such as succession planning? One complaint heard from human resource professionals is that in hard times, the succession plan goes out the window. Training and development programs are even more likely to meet the same fate during cutbacks, along with research and development and other investments in the future.

Therefore, let us consider the following questions:

11. How do mobility rates vary as a function of the growth rate of the organization? Is one possible "silver lining" of a slow-growth organization the fact that people stay longer in their assignments and have a chance to master them and recover from the negative effects of the last move? How do

the anti-plateauing measures proposed by Dewhirst relate to the growth rate of the organization?

12. Or, in a slow-growth or declining organization, is it even more important to keep people moving frequently, to prevent stagnation? (Of course, tight financial resources might make frequent moves impossible.)

Organizational Career Systems

As Morrison shows (chapter 2), there is both a "micro" side and a "macro" side to career development. The individual is ultimately responsible for making career decisions and dealing with the motivational issues related to managing his or her own work life in turbulent organizations over a long, uncertain future working life. Hicks and London (chapter 6) nicely describe how these individual decision and motivation processes do and should work. However, notwithstanding the individual's personal responsibility, it is the organization that represents the structure of future work opportunities and that controls many of the mobility processes we have discussed. The difficult issue here is, how can we get a better integration between individual career planning processes and organizational career management systems? We are in far better shape on this issue than we were in the mid-1970s (Hall, 1976).

Many more organizations have built in career discussions between managers and employees either as an add-on to the performance appraisal discussion, or as a separate periodic activity (Gutteridge, 1986). Succession planning systems are incorporating increasing amounts of information on candidates' career and mobility preferences. Career opportunity information, often through job posting, is becoming more open, even for higher level jobs.

One critical gap here is the lack of what I call *strategic human resource development* (Hall, 1986b). This is a process of identifying, from the strategic business plan, future managerial and technical skills that will be needed and devising and implementing plans for the development of those skills in the workforce. Specific details of how to make these strategic linkages in a career management system are described by Ford and Bhagat's (chapter 3).

Too often, the organization lacks planning in the area of developing people and is suddenly confronted with critical skill shortages in particular areas. Then massive external hiring is necessary, at high salary levels, and tremendous equity problems are created for present employees.

It may not be possible to forecast too precisely what skills will be needed in the future. If the strategic planning process is not perfect, then any other plans based on that will be even less accurate. Dewhirst (chapter 4) deals with the troublesome issue of assessing what mix of specialist versus generalist skills will be needed.

This is a key issue for the military, which needs large numbers of young "warriors" (line officers) and not so many senior ones, whereas the proportions are reversed for staff functions involved in acquiring large weapons systems (staff). One option is to consider hybrid specialists, people with a clear specialty area who then become trained in at least one other area, as well (Morrison & Wilcove, 1989). This way, there is more flexibility for the person and the organization, but not the disadvantage of the generalist model. Thus, as Hayes (1985) advocated, the organization would be developing a pool of resources that could then be applied to rapidly changing organizational objectives. He called this a reverse strategy process, planning from means to ends, rather than the more traditional forward strategic approach of working from ends to means. Let's state this as a question:

13. How can the organization better identify needed future skills and develop plans to "grow" those skills in people, rather than acquiring them externally later? A closely related issue at the organizational level is that of who gets developmental attention? In many organizations, most developmental resources are directed toward fast trackers (high potentials, stars, 5 percenters, etc.) Solid citizens, high-performing plateaued employees who represent the backbone of the organization and perform most of the real work of the organization, often have far fewer opportunities to attend seminars, receive developmental assignments, and the like (see Stoner, Ference, Warren, & Christensen, 1980). With slower promotion rates and flatter organizations, most attention in the future will have to be paid to the growth of the solid citizen. How can development be better built into the job itself? One company's answer, a project management career track, is discussed by Hall (1985). Another approach, which identifies different types of plateauing and the appropriate organizational actions for each, is provided by Kaye (1989).

Another critical system issue is the extent to which the organization devotes programmatic effort to developing the careers of individuals who are *different* from the white male group currently in key positions (i.e., people of color, women, ethnic minorities). A critical problem in the management development processes of most organizations is that the better the succession planning process is, the more severe is the problem of *executive cloning* (Hall, 1986b). And we know that with the growing diversity of the work force and global markets of the next century, the most adaptive organizations will be those whose top management mirrors that environmental diversity (Johnson & Packer, 1987).

Thus, the issue here is not simply affirmative action or "doing the right thing"; it is a matter of organizational adaptation and survival. (For the exceptional conceptual and review paper on this topic, see Thomas & Alderfer, 1989. Another major contribution here is a special edition of the *Journal of Organizational Behavior,* edited by Ella Louise Bell, 1990.)

14. What are the factors related to the barriers to and success of people of color and those representing other types of diversity in the work force? How do race and other differences affect individual careers and organizational career systems from the perspective of the individual, the group, intergroups, and the organization as a whole? How do programs to promote and value diversity relate to overall organizational effectiveness?

Organizational Trauma: "The Deal is Changing"

One of the undercurrents running through all of these chapters, and a comment heard often at the workshop was, "The deal is changing." The psychological contact between the individual and the employer is shifting. For the organization this means that the environment is less stable and predictable. Organizations like AT&T, IBM, automobile companies, insurance companies, and government agencies, which years ago represented the ultimate in stable environments, are now undergoing changes (cutbacks, new areas of business, new forms of competition, etc.) that severely threaten their corporate health. Many of the Fortune 500 companies from the 1950s do not exist any more, either because of mergers, acquisitions, restructuring, bankruptcy, or simply a decision to go out of business. The changing compositions of the airline, computer, and financial services industries are good cases in point here. The deal is also different in terms of employee loyalty; it is not there. Employees are now acting like "free agents," managing and directing their own careers in their own best interests. (of course, this is entirely rational and adaptive for the employee, given the turbulence in the organizational environment.) The baby boom cohort's moving into mid-career represents a significant force shaping these changes (Hall & Richter, 1990).

For the individual, this means new expectations, as well. Whereas, on entry, the "deal" was a long-term relationship with reasonable security if the person performed well and perhaps an expectation of rising to a certain level in the organization. Certainly, professionals and managers were not faced with the threat of being "laid off." In turn, the individual would show loyalty, work long hours, accept geographical moves willingly (because there would be a promotional payoff later, most likely.) Now companies traditionally known for long-term employment policies, such as Exxon and AT&T, have had to trim large percentages of their managerial and professional workforce, and the deal there has definitely changed. Question:

15. What is the new "deal?" What are the mutual expectations in the psychological contract between the individual and the organization? How is it being communicated? How can the organization support employees in making the necessary career adaptations?

Result: The Protean career

The result of the deal changing is that, in fact, employees are becoming more like free agents whose main resources are a set of skills that can serve them in a number of ways. Their skills can provide opportunities and security in their present organization.

These skills can be used to negotiate a better deal with the present employer, or if this is not successful, to strike a better arrangement across the street. The new deal reads like this: Security is in your career competencies. "Metaskills" such as adaptability and clear identity are the keys to effective self-management and career change.

Commitment is to one's skills and to one's professional work. If the present organization provides opportunities to practice and to develop one's professional skills, the person will develop loyalty to that organization. Thus, personal loyalty is not gone; it is just more conditional than in the past. There has to be mutual commitment, commitment by the organization to the person as well as from the person to the employer.

We are seeing now in practice what in the 1970s was a very budding phenomenon, the *protean career* (Hall, 1976, 1986a):

> The protean career is a process which the person, not the organization, is managing. It consists of all of the person's varied experiences in education, training, work in several organizations, changes in occupational field, etc. The protean career is not what happens to the person in any one organization. The protean person's own personal career choices and search for self-fulfillment are the unifying or integrative elements in his or her life. The criterion of success is internal (psychological success), not external. In short, the protean career is shaped more by the individual than by the organization and may be redirected from time to time to meet the needs of the person. (Hall, 1976, p. 201)

We see the protean career acknowledged at the organizational level when senior executives make statements such as, "The career is the individual's responsibility." In fact, such has always been the case; ultimately no one cares as much about a person's career as does that person him or herself. However, now this fact is being acknowledged, and organizational resources are being mobilized to support it.

It appears that certain skills are critical to a person in the process of being protean. These are skills in learning how to learn. I call them "metaskills." These include adaptability (routine busting), tolerance of ambiguity and uncertainty, self-awareness, and identity change (Hall, 1986a). The good news is that it appears that these and related skills can be developed (London & Stumpf, 1986).

The Hicks and London chapter provides more detail on the important issue of self-direction in the career. Their model of factors affecting career decision making represents an important way to integrate the various personal, organizational, and environmental factors that shape opportunities and the way they are perceived. Of all the factors in their model, it seems that the individual variables (e.g., decision style, career motivation, career strategies, nonwork responsibilities, values, and gender and identity group status) are most in need of research at this point.

A major question here deals with these individual difference factors: how much self-directed change an individual or organization can cope with. What proportion of the population can be protean in this way? Do some people react differently than others, and if so, how do we account for those differences? How do people learn from experience?

16. What exactly are the meta-skills involved in successful protean career management, and what methods are most effective in developing them?

Career as Transitions

The flexibility of the protean career style means that the career, to an increasing extent, will consist of a series of important transitions. Some of these will be job and role transitions, and others will be changes in work caused by transitions in one's personal life. Daniel Levinson (1986) has argued that approximately half of a person's adult life is spent in developmental transitions. We will need to know much most about the process of embracing surprise (Hall, 1986a) and mastering skills in sense-making (Louis, 1980). Louis (personal communication, 1986) argued that we now need to move beyond the individual transitioner and examine the significant others in that person's life: colleagues, family members, friends, in short the extra-role support system. We also need to examine the effects of the transition on the subset of these significant others who do not move.

We already know a bit about "survival guilt" among survivors of trauma (e.g., Brockner et al., 1986), and some of these concepts have been applied to organizational trauma, but much more research is needed.

The second need in studying transitions is to give more attention to the affective outcomes of the transition (Louis, personal communication, 1986). We now have good research on the cognitive and behavioral effects, as we have seen in Minor, Slade, and Meyer's chapter. Their model of the career transition process is extremely helpful.

We now need more work on the feelings and pain (e.g., excessive stress) associated with major disruptions in one's life. The relevance of affect is one reason executive education professionals give for the interest in Outward Bound-type survival training in executive development programs in companies such as General Electric and Kraft General Foods; it helps people deal with pain, recognize and mobilize personal coping resources, and develop interpersonal support systems. Thus, survival training is one human resource system response to organizational trauma.

In question form, then:

17. In what ways are significant others affected in a transition? How does this change in the transitioner's support system affect the support the person receives? What are the effects of the transition on nontransitioners?

18. Beyond looking at excess stress (which only gives us a global general measure of affect, and is thus a "dead-end"), what are the more fundamental dimensions of affect that are impacted by various types of transitions? What factors moderate these impacts? What role do significant others play in these relationships?

Needed Organizational Responses

What does all of this mean for organizations concerned with a humane and effective career management system? First, it means that *people have a tremendous need for information during organizational trauma.* Even if top management can only say what they do not know, it is important to be in communication with employees about what is happening. Unfortunately, senior managers, long socialized to come up with solutions to problems, feel uncomfortable when they do not have a solution or information, and they tend to avoid communication during periods of uncertainty.

There is a need for people to deal with their feelings about organizational turbulence ("emotional dumping" as one human resource development professional put it.) This is especially important for higher-level managers, who often are put in the role of the senior person who feels the need to act positive and in control. People at all levels in the organization need to have an opportunity to express their feelings about their careers.

For fast trackers, there is a need for the organization to "let them know you love them," as one human resource executive put it. This is especially true during organizational cutbacks. Top management cannot assume that high potential people know they are wanted when large numbers of people are being encouraged to leave.

For plateauers, the need for information should be met with realistic feedback on their career status. They should have counseling to help them come to terms with their feelings about their careers and to sort out what they want to do next. And they need coaching in how best to grow in the directions they want to take.

And finally, we need better research on career management programs to help provide these organizational career resources to individual employees. We need data on this question:

19. What are the organizational and personal effects of various design characteristics of career development programs for providing organizational and career information, emotional support, counseling, and coaching to employees? For example, what is the effectiveness of training line managers to perform some of these functions? What is the potential of personal computers or mass communication for providing organizational and personal information?

We need more study of the complex methodological issues in studying such career program effects, especially when the research is longitudinal, as it should be in many cases of career processes. This is because the more complex the research becomes, the more a particular design or analysis decision can affect the results, and thus the study's policy implications. The more consensus we can obtain about methods of career research, the more of a "common currency" of understanding of career dynamics we will have about appropriate career interventions.

There are also equally complex research designs and analytic methods available for studying life-span development (e.g., cross-sequential designs, structural regression analysis). The issue of reactive effects in longitudinal research (e.g., the effect of knowing that one is being assessed) is critical and has not yet been adequately addressed. Most managers are probably aware that the process of studying a phenomenon changes that phenomenon, but we do not know what that implies for career research. It could be that the effects are positive, in the sense of a Hawthorne Effect. That is, doing research on a person's career implies organization interest in the person's development. If so, a key factor would be taking action to make changes based on the research findings.

Different types of stability (structural, mean level, and intra-individual) are key concerns, especially when we are looking for change. One would expect to find instability at all three levels when studying developmental processes. This raises the issue of when are we finding true change and when are we simply encountering measurement problems?

A final issue deals with the career management system (policies and practices involving the use of the corporate structure in developing and utilizing people.) Most of our research on career management systems, such as succession planning programs or assessment centers, describes their effectiveness in terms of individual-level outcomes, not organizational level outcomes. That is, a given study might describe the effectiveness of, say, an assessment center in terms of its ability to predict which candidates would reach a certain level of management within a certain period of time (e.g., Wingrove, Jones, & Herriot, 1985.) However, we need more research on the impact of career management systems on the overall effectiveness of the organization. The first research of this type, to my knowledge, is being conducted by Friedman (1986) on succession planning systems. The integrative model of corporate and career development strategies provided here by Morrison represents an important and novel step in building theory in this area. There has been much discussion of the need to integrate business strategy with human resource development strategy, and this chapter gives clear specific detail on how to do it. Other relevant work linking strategy to career development is found in Slocum, Cron, Hansen, and Rawlings (1985); Sonnenfeld (1989); and Hall (1989).

Thus, our final question is:

20. What impact do career management systems have on the overall effectiveness of the organization? For example, what is the effectiveness of alternative forms of job progression or succession planning on an organization's ability to remain flexible and reach its goals (Morrison & Hock, 1986)? What are the effects on organizational performance of programs for valuing diversity and the promotion of different types of managers (i.e., non-White, male candidates)? What are the organizational-wide effects of the installation of a human resource information system or a manager-driven career coaching and counseling program?

SUMMARY

Many of the questions raised here deal with the interface between macro (organizational) activities and micro (individual) career activities. The real "action" in organizational careers these days is in the cognitive and affective response areas. However, the most potent "triggers" to these responses are actions taken at the organizational level. The best emerging work on careers will merge these two perspectives (Arthur, Hall, & Lawrence, 1989a). The more we learn about this complex area, the more we find we need to know.

In particular, we have seen how the issue of job mobility is a key link between organization career actions and individual career experience. As organizations become more global, requiring even more diverse forms of movement, the need for good research is growing accordingly. Another key link that needs more attention is that between career and family (or work–life balance). It is now becoming clearer to organizations that this is a *business* issue, not just a personal concern for employees. It is also clear that careers are becoming more flexible or *protean*, so that a focus on transitions is a good way to capture critical events in the career.

This brings us to the final area of questions for the future: What are the appropriate responses of the organization to create more effective career management and career development? This requires careful empirical examination of organizational practices that already have been tried and of experiments with innovative approaches. Studying these fast-moving, adaptive processes may require correspondingly flexible qualitative or in-depth case study approaches to supplement more traditional quantitative methods.

REFERENCES

Arthur, M. B., Hall, D. T., & Lawrence, B. S. (1989a). Generating new directions in career theory: The case for a transdisciplinary approach. In M. B. Arthur, D. T. Hall, & B. S. Lawrence (Eds.), *Handbook of career theory* (pp. 7–25). Cambridge, England: Cambridge University Press.

Arthur, M. B., Hall, D. T., & Lawrence, B. S. (Eds.). (1989b). *Handbook of career theory.* Cambridge, England: Cambridge University Press.

Bell, E. L. (in press). Introduction to the special edition on the career and life process of black professionals. *Journal of Organizational Behavior.*

Brett, J. (1982). Job transfer and well-being. *Journal of Applied Psychology, 67,* 450–463.

Brockner, J., Greenberg, J., Brockner, A., Bortz, J., Davy, J., & Carter, C. (1986). Layoffs, equity theory, and work performance: Further evidence of the impact of survivor guilt. *Academy Of Management Journal, 29,* 373–384.

Brown, D., Brooks, L., & Associates (1990). *Career choice and development: Applying contemporary theories to practice* (2nd ed.). San Francisco: Jossey-Bass.

Friedman, S. D. (1986). Succession systems in large corporations: Characteristics and correlates of performance. *Human Resource Management, 25,* 191–213.

Greenhaus, J. H., & Beutell, N. J. (1985). Sources of conflict between work and family roles. *Academy of Management Review, 10,* 76–88.

Greenhaus, J. H., & Parasuraman, S. (1986). Vocational and organizational behavior, 1985: A review. *Journal of Vocational Behavior, 29,* 115–176.

Gutteridge, T. G. (1986). Organizational career development systems: The state of the practice. In D. T. Hall and Associates, (Eds.), *Career development in organizations* (pp. 50–94). San Francisco: Jossey-Bass.

Hall, D. T. (1976). *Careers in organizations.* Glenview, IL: Scott Foresman.

Hall, D. T. (1981). Socialization processes in later career years: Can there be growth at the terminal level? In C. B. Derr (Ed.), *Work, family, and the career* (pp. 219–233). New York: Praeger.

Hall, D. T. (1985). Project work as an antidote to career plateauing in a declining engineering organization. *Human Resource Management, 24,* 271–292.

Hall, D. T. (1986a). Breaking career routines: Midcareer choice and identity development. In D. T. Hall and Associates (Eds.), *Career development in organizations* (pp. 120–159). San Francisco: Jossey-Bass.

Hall, D. T. (1986b). Dilemmas in linking succession planning to individual executive learning. *Human Resource Management, 25,* 235–265.

Hall, D. T. (1989). How top management and the organization itself can block effective executive succession. *Human Resource Management, 28,* 5–24.

Hall, D. T. (1990). Promoting work/family balance: An organization-change approach. *Organizational Dynamics, 18,* 5–18.

Hall, D. T., & Goodale, J. G. (1986). *Human resource management: Strategy, design, and implementation.* Glenview, IL: Scott, Foresman.

Hall, D. T., & Richter, J. (1988). Balancing work life and home life: What can organizations do to help? *The Academy of Management Executive, 11,* 213–223.

Hall, D. T., & Richter, J. (1990). Career gridlock: Baby boomers hit the wall. *Academy Of Management Executive, 4,* 7–22.

Hayes, R. H. (1985). Strategic planning—Forward or reverse? *Harvard Business Review, 63,* 111–119.

Johnson, W. B., & Packer, A. E. (1987). *Workforce 2000: Work and workers for the twenty-first century.* Indianapolis, IN: Hudson Institute.

Katz, R. (1978). Job longevity as a situational factor in job satisfaction. *Administrative Science Quarterly, 23,* 204–223.

Kaye, B. L. (1989). Plateaued performers: Choices and challenges. New York, NY: The Center for Career Research and Human Resources Management, Columbia University.

Levinson, D. J. (1986). A conception of adult development. *American Psychologist. 41,* 3–13.

London, M., & Stumpf, S. A. (1986). Individual and organizational career development in changing times. In D. T. Hall and Associates (Eds.), *Career development in organizations* (pp. 21–49). San Francisco: Jossey-Bass.

Louis, M. R. (1980). Surprise and sense making: What newcomers experience in entering unfamiliar organizational settings. *Administrative Science Quarterly, 25,* 226–251.

McCall, M. W., Jr., Lombardo, M., & Morrison, A. M. (1988). *The lessons of experience.* Lexington, MA: Lexington Books.

Morrison, R. F., & Hock, R. R. (1986). Career building: Learning from cumulative work experience. In D. T. Hall and Associates (Eds.), *Career development in organizations* (pp. 236–273). San Francisco: Jossey-Bass.

Morrison, R. F., & Wilcove, G. L. (1989 August). Roadblocks to warrior subspecialty development. In M. F. Wiskoff (Chair), *Aspects of Navy Work and development.* Symposium conducted at the meeting of the American Psychological Association, New Orleans, August.

Nicholson, N., & West, M. (1989). Transitions, work histories, and careers. In M. B. Arthur, D. T. Hall, & B. S. Lawrence (Eds.), *Handbook of career theory* (pp. 181–201). Cambridge, England: Cambridge University Press.

Richter, J. (1983). *The daily transitions between professional and private life.* Unpublished doctoral dissertation, Boston University, Boston, MA.

Slocum, J. W. Jr., Cron, W. L., Hansen, R. W., & Rawlings, S. (1985). Business strategy and the management of plateaued employees. *Academy of Management Journal, 28,* 133–154.

Sonnenfeld, J. (1989). Career system profiles and strategic staffing. In M. B. Arthur, D. T. Hall, & B. S. Lawrence (Eds.), *Handbook of career theory* (pp. 202–224). Cambridge, England: Cambridge University Press.

Stoner, J. A. F., Ference, T. P., Warren, E. K., & Christensen, H. K. (1980). *Managerial career plateaus.* New York: Center for Research in Career Development, Columbia University.

Thomas, D. A., & Alderfer, C. P. (1989). The influence of race and career dynamics: Theory and research on minority career experiences. In M. B. Arthur, D. T. Hall, & B. S. Lawrence (Eds.), *Handbook of career theory* (pp. 133–158). Cambridge, England: Cambridge University Press.

University of San Diego. (1984). *Proceedings: Volume 1. Group Reports. Tri-Service Career Research Workshop.* San Diego, CA: Author.

Veiga, J. F. (1981). Plateaued versus nonplateaued managers: Career patterns, attitudes, and path potential. *Academy of Management Journal, 24,* 566–578.

Voyandoff, P. (1988). Work and family: A review and expanded conceptualization. *Journal of Social Behavior and Personality, 3,* 1–22.

Wingrove, J., Jones, A. & Herriot (1985). The predictive validity of pre- and post-discussion assessment centre ratings. *Journal of Occupational Psychology, 58,* 189–192.

Author Index

Subject Index